ENCOUNTERS
—WITH—
WISDOM

❖ BOOK TWO ❖

ENCOUNTERS
—WITH—
WISDOM

❖ BOOK TWO ❖

Thomas Hora, M.D.

The PAGL Foundation
Old Lyme, CT

Published by the PAGL Foundation
P.O. Box 4001, Old Lyme, CT 06371

Copyright © 2007 by the PAGL Foundation.

Manufactured in the United States of America.

Library of Congress Cataloging-in-Publication Data

ISBN: 1-978-1-93105-204-7
Library of Congress Control Number: 2007928533

Contents

Introduction   7

1. Radical Therapy   9

2. Is You Is or Is You Ain't?   24

3. Freedom and Corruptibility   39

4. Wanting to Be Right   56

5. The Wisdom to Know the Difference   74

6. Reaction vs. Response   89

7. The Greatest Protection   107

8. Reverence for Life   123

Introduction

This book is the second in a series of short volumes that continue to present Dr. Thomas Hora's Metapsychiatric teachings through dialogues with his students. Dr. Hora, the founder of Existential Metapsychiatry, was a pioneering psychiatrist whose work provided hermeneutic clarification of psychological issues in the larger context of existential and spiritual wisdom and understanding. He passed away in 1995, and his work lives on.

This selection of dialogues from the 1980s and 1990s remains fresh and helpful. We are fortunate that Dr. Hora tape-recorded most of his weekly group sessions with his students and made them available to those who were there. The Board of the PAGL Foundation* has collected many of the tapes and transcribed some of them. They have then been carefully edited to guarantee participant anonymity, improve readability, coherence and relevance, and to assign a title to each based on the principal theme of each meeting.

---

*PAGL is an acronym for Peace, Assurance, Gratitude, and Love, qualities of consciousness that are the fruit of spiritual progress. The PAGL Foundation was established to make the work of Dr. Hora available. Previously published books consisting of group dialogues are *Dialogues in Metapsychiatry* and *One Mind*. Basic books by Dr. Hora on Existential Metapsychiatry are *Beyond the Dream* and *Existential Metapsychiatry*. These and other books and tapes are available from the PAGL Foundation and its bookstore (see *www.pagl.org*).

At each session Dr. Hora would enter the room and sit at the front of a circle of students. He would quietly look around the room, smiling at each participant. Someone would begin by asking a question or presenting a problem. Sometimes no one spoke up and Dr. Hora began by seeking to discern what was on peoples' minds.

The dialogue proceeded with Dr. Hora encouraging the students to shed light on whatever issue had been raised, and shifted when some participant found the need to bring up another topic. Everything flowed, and there was never pressure to continue discussing any single issue. At the end of each session the students left with a new understanding.

Encounters in Wisdom is your invitation to join that dialogue.

Radical Therapy

Student: Dr. Hora, I've had this sore throat for a while now. It seems to come and go. I can't understand my reluctance to face up to the meaning of it and to get beyond it. I don't know if I don't understand the meaning or if I am reluctant to be healed.

Dr. Hora: Well, do you want to be healed of the sore throat or do you want to be healed of the meaning of the sore throat? Usually, when we have a painful symptom, we want to get rid of the symptom, and then we get into trouble because the symptom is just a thought. Unless we are willing to face up to the 3 Rs, then we are just looking for relief — fast, fast, relief. Take an Anacin, or two, and then call the doctor in the morning. Now let's remember that Metapsychiatry teaches that every physical symptom is an interaction thought. It's coming and it's going... right? When Satan was asked, "Who are you? Where do you come from?" he said, "I am the one that goes up and down and to and fro in the world" (Job 1:7; 2:2). What does that mean? How can a symptom come and go? Is it a commuter system? Either it is or it ain't. Is you is or is you ain't? So we have to ask two intelligent questions. Did you ask them?

Student: Maybe not sincerely.

Dr. Hora: Okay, so go home and ask sincerely. Yes, we don't want to bother with this Metapsychiatric stuff. Just give me something so the pain will go away. So it is much more practical to rely on traditional medicine. Give me a syrup of some kind or a pill, and it will relieve the pain. But it will come back. So it's going and it's coming. Whenever a problem doesn't seem to yield, it is indicative that we don't want to face up to a certain thought, and we are looking not for a healing but for relief.

Student: What about the case where we have a cold, and we see the meaning and it goes away and we realize that we replaced the thought with a valid thought. But then it comes again. Did we just kid ourselves the first time?

Dr. Hora: Sure. Of course. We do that all the time. This is very radical therapy.

Student: Well, if it was healed temporarily, isn't distraction enough to heal the symptom?

Dr. Hora: Sure, you go to the movies and you come home and feel much better for awhile.

Student: Understanding is not transient, right?

Dr. Hora: True understanding is permanent.

Student: When you think that something is unable to be healed, when you think about why it isn't healing, suddenly it feels like blame, like "Oh, I didn't try hard enough," or "I didn't do this or something to find the meaning." I wondered if something like a cold, and given that it's February, could the meaning be so vague as that in the sea of mental garbage, everybody believes that colds are inevitable?

Dr. Hora: Yes, in February it is all right because God is in Florida. (laughter)

Student: I suppose my question is that when an individual suffers from something like a sore throat, does it have to be a specific meaning related to their mode of being-in-the-world or could it just simply be that they got caught in the net of this world-wide belief that people . . .

Dr. Hora: Wouldn't it be helpful to say that? (laughter) You are trying to avoid facing up to the real issues.

Student: But certain symptoms or mental habits are contagious, aren't they (e.g. fear)? If we read the newspapers about fearful things and we are inundated, or we are in an environment in which people are mentioning all kinds of fearful things, then we can succumb to that.

Dr. Hora: Yes, so?

Student: In other words, we are making a decision to pay attention to that kind of thinking. We have personal responsibility in a sense, but . . .

Dr. Hora: Give us an example.

Student: The one that was brought up about you catching a cold from everybody around you saying that they've got a cold. This one has a cold and I just believe that's the cause rather than some interaction thought which is really the underlying meaning of such a symptom. So if one wasn't experiencing interaction thinking, then one is unlikely, no matter how many people are coughing and sneezing around you, to succumb.

Dr. Hora: Well, suppose somebody has a sore throat because he is sore at his girlfriend, who is very Jewish or something. Now he has this sore throat and he keeps complaining to people at the workplace or in the family how this sore throat is annoying him. And he has it, and he can't get rid of it. And he describes the symptoms and here and there, some-how, his friends and relatives listen to the description of the symptoms, and, suddenly, they develop the same symptoms and they don't even know this Jewish girl. And they have the same symptoms as the original one who has the legitimate source.

Student: An interaction based sore throat. (laughter)

Dr. Hora: Right. Now what does that say?

Student: They have their own individual meaning for their sore throats.

Dr. Hora: Exactly. They just borrow the symptom. We bor-row, like the banking system; we can borrow not only money but symptoms too, and diseases. Then we say it is something going around. Now, when we say that we are saying, "This is contagious," the sore throat that he got from interaction with his girl is now an epidemic . . . right? Okay. So you don't have to have a fight with your girlfriend to get a sore throat. It's enough to sympathize with somebody, and many people can catch all kinds of diseases, and scientific studies make the claim that there is an epidemic of sore throats in February. Now we have to ask the meaning of contagion. How is it possible that we are subject to being affected by contagion? What makes us susceptible to contagion?

Student: The desire for self-confirmation.

Dr. Hora: Exactly. We are always interested in having something that would confirm our individuality by imitating others: individuality through conformity. Isn't that interesting? So epidemics and contagions are just indicating that a vast majority of people live in a state of fear or resentment and are susceptible to borrowing symptoms with which they can say, "Me too." From early childhood on we keep saying, "Me too." This is the human condition. It still has a meaning. Now, on television the pharmaceutical industries have discovered that it's wonderful if you want to sell some kind of medicine. First you have to hire good actors who will portray the hemorrhoids or whatever they want to sell. So they make people get sick, through demonstrating what it feels like to experience that particular illness. You see all kinds of things on television. They show you how to be sick, and then they show you how to buy the medicine that purportedly is going to remove this sickness. You're almost like God. The Lord giveth and the Lord taketh away. This is the national health care system. And it is public education. The public is being educated how to be sick and how to buy the medicines that will relieve you.

You can see all kinds of diseases on television. Whatever turns you on, you can see and you can buy it and you hope that by July you will be all right because the weather will change. Not long ago there was an epidemic of swine flu and a panic in Congress about it. Do you remember the epidemic of swine flu? They spent millions of dollars to get the vaccine against the flu and the more they talked about how to pre-vent the swine flu, the more people were in fear of getting the swine flu. Something happened. Within a few weeks nobody spoke about it. Once the vaccine was available there was no more swine flu. And the millions of dollars that were given to the pharmaceutical companies to prepare this vaccine were all spent. So we are just doing all kinds of things and getting poorer all the time. We're becoming economically exhausted. We are exhausting ourselves in futile and invalid methods of protecting the public, and protecting ourselves. It's a fantastic comedy of errors...when the scientific discoveries are pre-sented as a panacea that will protect us. There are all kinds of medications. It is just amazing. What were people doing when there was no pharmaceutical industry? And they also lived to be 90–95. My grandfather never went to the doctor and he never went to the dentist and he lived to be 94. He was just an average vineyard owner. They made wine; maybe that helped. (laughter) It was lousy wine, sour...like vinegar. (laughter)

Student: Where do you separate the interaction thought from the self-confirmatory?

Dr. Hora: No need to separate them. They are practically the same. It's always the self-confirmatory thought that comes to us in one form or another and makes us eager to receive any kind of symptom that happens to be in vogue. It's like the fashion industry that presents all kinds of things to the public, which buys it because it's the trend. We are very trendy people. We buy electronics, we buy clothes, we buy food, or whatever is in vogue. I noticed that Mrs. Clinton appeared a few days ago with a scarf all the way up to the neck like this.

Two days later, on television, you could see women wearing scarves the same way. Whether it is appealing or not doesn't matter, nor whether it is good or nice looking. No, it's "Me too." Now thousands of women will wear scarves up to their chin like that, in March. They still do it. Well, that's at least an innocent kind of self-confirmation. But to get sick in order to be fashionable is really stupid.

Student: How do we lose interest in self-confirmation without having a sense that we are giving something up?

Dr. Hora: We must never think about giving something up. In principle, we don't give anything up. But we can be interested in finding something that is more valid and good and health-promoting and happifying. You don't have to give up a sore throat. No, you just have to find spiritual blessedness. You can keep your sore throat, but you have to become interested in something that is really good, and you don't have to struggle in giving up the bad. It never was anything. There are some religious groups throughout the world who call themselves the Renunciates, and they are constantly focusing attention on how to sacrifice and renounce everything that is pleasurable or painful. They want to renounce what the whole world is interested in. That isn't going to help. God doesn't ask you to get rid of your sore throat. He doesn't even know that there is such a thing. And when you try to get rid of the sore throat, you get worse, and when religion preaches renunciation, then it is guiding you into a negative blind alley. It is called an anti-hedonistic orientation. No, it is not necessary to get rid of your sore throat. What is needed is to be interested in happiness and spiritual blessedness and freedom and joy and perfect love. We do not have to make 2 and 2 to not be 5. We don't have to get rid of the 5. It ain't nothing anyway. We just have to be interested in knowing the truth.

We don't get rewarded for suffering. This is also a misguided religious notion that the more you suffer, the greater your reward will be. You could all see in Iran, when they were demonstrating in the streets, the religious fanatics were beating themselves with chains, showing naked bodies and the blood was flowing from their bodies. What were they doing? They were bribing God with suffering. This is also a crazy religious idea, that you earn rewards from God by suffering. It's good for you, and God enjoys watching you grieve and suffer. What kind of monster is that? God is not interested in suffering. God is love. God is freedom. God is joy. God is beauty. God is intelligence. Some people are afraid to be happy. Do you know that? That God may get jealous if you are happy. God is a jealous god and a sadistic god. We have all kinds of Gods...but not in Metapsychiatry.

Student: Let's say that you realize that you are clinging to something that's hurting you and we know that's the meaning. But we say that we don't have to give it up, so...

Dr. Hora: Enjoy it while you can. (laughter)

Student: So then will God liberate us? So let's say that we realize that we have to give it up...but it is so engrained.

Dr. Hora: Yes, you cannot give it up. It's not possible. And then when you try to give it up you are giving it reality and honoring it as a power. And you get embroiled in this struggle.

Student: So how do you get liberated from that quagmire, because we all have our own little things.

Dr. Hora: Have you ever heard that we are more interested in getting rid of the symptom than in knowing the truth?

Student: So we never really face the issue.

Dr. Hora: Of course. You cannot be interested in two things at the same time. Jesus said you cannot serve two masters; you will like the one and hate the other or vice versa.

Student: You cannot reorient without understanding the meaning first. You can't just transcend your thought without understanding.

Dr. Hora: If you can stand on the left foot for a long time and it's raining outside, then maybe you can.

Student: So the first thing is understanding the meaning?

Dr. Hora: Yes, right. But don't get attached to it. Sometimes you can get attached to the meaning and perpetuate the symptom. We have to primarily work with the first principle. We are interested in the good of God rather than in the evil of a disease or a problem or anything else. "Thou shalt have no other interests before the good of God, which is spiritual blessedness." Now suppose you are feeling low and you say, "Well I want to have some fun and feel good. I'll go to a bar and pick up a girl and have a few drinks and I'll enjoy life." What would God say? Would God object to this? After all, you're interested in the good. It may not be the right kind of good. The right kind of good is not self-confirmatory. It is God-confirmatory. When we go to a bar to feel better, we're concerned with self-confirmation — right? And God says in the Bible, I have made you for myself... not for yourself... that ye may show forth my praise — not your own praise. ["This people have

I formed for myself; they shall shew forth my praise" (Isaiah 43:21).] This is the difficulty, that we are more interested in being here for ourselves rather than in being here for God. There is a universal desire for self-confirmatory experiences. We tend to do everything for ourselves. Sometimes we do it for others, but it's still not for God. How to be here for God without dissimulation, pretending, or such things.

Student: We read in the Bible that we can be transformed by the renewing of the mind. How can we really understand that? It seems the good of God is not something you can think knowingly about.

Dr. Hora: Oh yes, sure. Suppose you are having a whisky sour and you think about God. You say, "God gave us the whiskey sour; it must be right. Let's celebrate the idea of God by drinking the whiskey sour." But the first principle specifies what is the real, divine good. What is the specific good of God which the first principle specifies?

Student: Spiritual blessedness.

Dr. Hora: Spiritual blessedness. It's not the same as getting drunk. Neither alcohol, nor drugs, nor food, nor anything else. What is spiritual blessedness?

Student: PAGL.

Dr. Hora: What is PAGL?

Student: Spiritual blessedness. (laughter)

Dr. Hora: This is called circular reasoning.

Student: Is it the awareness that God is providing us with everything we need moment to moment, that God is guiding us in life?

Dr. Hora: Now how could we know that?

Student: Well, we have to be looking for it all the time, and when we look sincerely, it happens. We can't make it happen, and it doesn't happen if our motivation isn't pure.

Student: God works in surprising ways. Harmony happens. Things just work out well.

Dr. Hora: Yes, well it happens to people. Suppose you go to the horse races and things are working out good for you . . . right? Is this spiritual blessedness?

Student: It has a flip side.

Dr. Hora: It has a flip side, like what?

Student: Well, it's not just the results; it's the process. If one doesn't have the ongoing abiding interest in seeing God, even if something good happens, it's really meaningless in the long run.

Dr. Hora: How does the Bible describe that positive attitude toward spiritual blessedness?

Student: What occurs to me is, "Thou shalt keep him in perfect peace, whose mind is stayed on thee" (Isaiah 26:3).

Dr. Hora: That's good. Peace, of course, is very good. But at one point the Bible says, "He that seeketh findeth; he that knocketh, to him it shall be opened," and the third one is "He that asketh, receiveth" (Matthew 7:8). In other words, we have to cultivate a positive, receptive attitude toward the good of God by seeking, knocking, and asking. And we discover that indeed there is such a thing as spiritual blessedness. We become peaceful, loving, happy, healthy, fearless, surprisingly intelligent, articulate. All kinds of good things can come . . . until we watch television and things start to go downhill.

Student: What you said before, that the good can only be God-confirmatory, was very helpful. There can't be any good emanating from the self.

Dr. Hora: Right.

Student: It seems that there can be good, but it's fake good. It's not real. It just seems like it's good, but it's not.

Dr. Hora: It's self-confirmatory.

Student: Something good can happen and you think it's good, but it's not confirming God in any way. It's confirming your self. It's easy to think that it could be good but never question whether this is confirming me or God.

Dr. Hora: That's the rub. It's all for the pursuit of happiness, which is in our Constitution. We have a right to pursue happiness, and most of us do it . . .

Student: . . . in all the wrong places.

Dr. Hora: It is very good to contemplate spiritual blessedness frequently, so that we have a very clear understanding of what is really good. Most people don't know it. They think if I feel good that's good; but it's not necessarily so.

Student: A couple of weeks ago, we were talking in a private session about spiritual blessedness. I said to you something like, "Is the definition of spiritual blessedness that one is aware that all things work together for good?" Every time I thought of that, I couldn't see how the working out of daily activity could be spiritual blessedness, because spiritual blessedness seems to refer to an intangible something. The working out of our daily activities or interests is tangible, and we can talk about it. And you said something that helped me understand it very well. You said, "Where does the energy come from that allows you to participate in life? Where does the intelligence come from? Where does the creativity come from? Where does the peace come from that helps these things work together for good? All of these qualities are coming from God into our experience." So if these are the qualities which are defining spiritual blessedness and making that definition valid, not so much that is tangible is working out. I had never thought of it that way, and all of a sudden, it opened my understanding up. If there is nothing more important than spiritual blessedness, you really need to understand what it is. And it always seemed to be something I could say and say, but I could never pierce the idea so that I could understand it.

Dr. Hora: It can come to us if we are sincerely contemplating what it is and how one could know it. We have the great blessing of having the definition of spiritual blessedness and perfect love. It is a well kept secret — perfect love. Most people have no idea what it is. So we can positively identify it and that is a protection against misunderstanding. Ignorance and misunderstanding are dangerous. It is very important to have very clear definitions and to clarify what it is we are talking about, even though it is somewhat intangible. But it is possible to know the truth which sets us free and heals us and liberates us. Last week we were talking about freedom and the fear of freedom. Do you remember?

Student: Dr. Hora, regarding the issue of freedom, I was wondering if phenomenology contributes to freedom in the sense that it gives the ability to see moment to moment without putting it into a context that immediately clouds your ability to see the issues. I guess it is the idea of bracketing. And if we could always in our lives take everything that comes into our path and see it without our preconceived ideas, then this would be freedom.

Dr. Hora: Well this would help us to be more understanding of issues. Phenomenology is not directly related to spirituality. It is a method of obtaining the open mind in order to understand things, what people say, and what is happening or what we are experiencing. We need the open mind, and phenomenology is a method whereby we can learn to confront reality or misstatements about reality with an open mind. It is very tragic when two people are talking and they are thinking about entirely different things. And they are pretending to talk to each other, but they are not really there. There is a lot of pretending and everybody has his own private agenda, even when they are talking about seemingly the same thing. It is a miserable condition if we don't have the ability to really listen to somebody else. You pretend to listen, but you have your own thoughts to think. Now through training in phenomenology we learn the open-minded confrontation of issues in life. If somebody is reporting to you about the weather, you hear what he is saying. You are not pretending to hear while you are thinking about baseball or something like that. This goes on all the time. People don't pay attention to each other. They pretend to communicate, but they are really not there. Children in the schools pretend that they are paying attention to what the teacher is saying, and all the time they are doing something else. Then when they are called to the blackboard, they don't know anything. They were not paying attention. Thinking is an obstacle to hearing. Did you know that? Thinking interferes with hearing. In some families, certain members develop hearing difficulties, and can even go completely deaf, because they don't want to hear what somebody is saying. They prefer to think their own thoughts.

Student: The reason I thought about that was that in thinking about freedom, you realize that as you go through the day, whether it is the people that you meet or new situations, it seems almost impossible to listen, to hear, because you bring all these preconceived ideas or whatever. It would seem to be a form of freedom to be able to experience things from moment to moment without the burden of parental guidelines so that your vision is very narrow.

Dr. Hora: It is the problem of attentiveness, being able to pay attention. I think in the schools they are trying to find some organic brain disease which would explain that certain children are unable to pay attention to the teacher. I believe it is called attention deficiency syndrome . . .

Student: It is called attention deficit disorder.

Dr. Hora: Yes, it is very scientific.

Student: You mean it's not just a boring teacher. (laughter)

2

Is You Is or Is You Ain't?

Student: What is the meaning of always wanting to be in another place than the place that I am at the moment? When I am doing one thing, I am thinking about the next thing that has to be done. I have great impatience with the present, whatever it is. Could we talk about this?

Dr. Hora: Sure, give us an example.

Student: Well, I could be sitting here thinking about what I am going to do after I leave the meeting tonight, instead of thinking about what we are talking about.

Dr. Hora: Well, the folklore says that we have "ants in our pants." (laughter) What is the meaning of having ants in our pants?

Student: I am glad you asked the question, because I have a similar question.

Dr. Hora: You too? (laughter)

Student: All that comes to mind is the idea of being ambitious, because ambition is involved with being preoccupied with the future, isn't it?

Dr. Hora: Well it could be, but not exactly.

Student: Can it be trying to feel good, because you don't feel so hot with doing this? So maybe the next thing will make you feel better.

Dr. Hora: That's a little closer. Yes, it is simply being negative in the now. When we're in the habit of negative thinking, we are always griping about now and hoping that after this there will be something better. "Ants in the pants" is a particular form of negative thinking based on the habit of griping. This is no good; that is no good; maybe that is going to be better. Of course this is nonsense, because God is omnipresent, infinite happiness, and goodness. To the extent that we understand it, we are grateful every moment of life. And oddly enough, things go from good to better. We become more and more grateful and happy. Things go well, and we glow with love. Life is good because life is God, the principle of infinite goodness. The more grateful we are, instead of griping, the more joyful we become, the more intelligent we become, and that is the enlightened way. Griping has never improved our situation, nor anybody's situation.

There is a story in the Bible, where a woman lost her child. He died in her arms (2 Kings 4:8–37). She put the child down on the bed and started running to see Elisha, the rabbi. Elisha saw her coming from a distance and said to her, "How is it with you?" And she said, "Well, all is well." And then the rabbi saw that something was troubling her. So she said, "Come to my house and see." So he came to her house and saw that the child was dead. So he said to the mother, "Leave me with the child, alone, in the room." And as the child was lying on the bed, he threw himself over the child and prayed,

and the child revived and he brought him out to the mother
and said, "Here, your son is alive."

It is an interesting story. The mother did not want to say
the bad thing, that the child had died, and that something
evil had happened to her. She said, "It is well." When we
are thinking negatively, we aggravate the situation instead
of helping. So under no circumstances is it helpful to gripe,
to complain, to kvetch, or to entertain hopelessly negative
thoughts. God is infinite Love-Intelligence, so how can there
be anything wrong or negative? Today there is an epidemic
of AIDS, of tuberculosis, of all kinds of illnesses, and there
is economic kvetching, world wide kvetching over the economy, people going into bankruptcies, and thousands of people
losing their jobs. Everything seems to be going from bad to
worse and everybody is catching the bug of complaining. And
the more people complain, the worse things get. There will
come a time when they will wake up and say, "What the hell
are we griping about so much? Let's become positive thinkers
and let's look at life from the perspective of God, the infinite
source of goodness." When that happens, we will see that the
recession will be over and things will be good again. And we'll
sing "Happy days are here again." (laughter)

Is the recession a material problem? No it's a mental problem. Unfortunately, all human problems have a tendency to
be contagious. What makes them contagious?

Student: Fear?

Student: Fascination with evil?

Dr. Hora: Fascination with evil is also contagious.

Student: It's self-confirmation.

Dr. Hora: Right! Problems, suffering, complaining, griping, kvetching. If you have an excuse to indulge in these negative modes of expression, they are secret ways of confirming oneself. We can confirm ourselves positively or negatively, and the easiest way to confirm ourselves is negatively. When things go well, we cannot take credit for that. We have to give credit to God. But if things go badly, we can say, "Well, I did it." We can take credit for the bad things in life unabashedly. Most people will not blame you for it. They will feel sorry for you and make you feel sicker than before. So illnesses, unhappiness, and disasters are more contagious than happiness, because it is easier to take credit for the bad things. You have to be blatantly egotistical to take credit for the good things in life. Anybody can tell you that you're just praising yourself. Therefore, we prefer to be sick, to be unhappy, to have problems, because then we can really take credit unabashedly. "Poor me." My father used to say, "I am most sincerely sorry for myself." (laughter) It was a standing joke.

Student: In this story, she was saying that all is well, but she didn't really know anything. The healing came through him.

Dr. Hora: Yes.

Student: But she knew enough to run to him.

Dr. Hora: Right. She ran to him, and he knew enough to go and pay a visit. Nowadays you can't even get a plumber or home visits. (laughter)

Student: So it was a form of worship that she was running to him. That was the highest form that she knew, to run to the rabbi.

Dr. Hora: She also knew that it was not right to complain, even at the point of such tragedy. She didn't want to say, "Oh, a horrible thing has happened." She wasn't crying. Notwithstanding appearances, all is well because God is infinite presence.

Student: Well, she didn't know that... right?

Dr. Hora: Well, apparently she was a disciple of the rabbi. She understood the teachings of the rabbi.

Student: So it isn't enough to know that complaining is not helpful.

Dr. Hora: No, but she knew enough to say, "All is well," and that was a very startling statement in this situation.

Student: So it indicates a state of receptivity.

Dr. Hora: Yes, because whenever we are griping, complaining, kvetching, bellyaching, or bullshitting, we are not only saying, "I am miserable." We are also saying, "There ain't no God; there is only evil." If there is a God, then only good can be. In divine reality there are no problems and no sicknesses. There is no need to run somewhere else to find happiness in the next town or in California. There is no need to go anywhere. We are already in the presence of God. So not only is it a self-confirmatory error to complain, but it is also a denial of the reality of God's good.

Student: There was a teacher that I knew last year and the year before, who in both years had what most people would consider a terrible class with many problems. I was always impressed with what wonders she seemed to work with the children, how they were so helpful and generous to each other, and how they didn't fight. Everything was so harmonious. And now, with your saying this, I recall that she never spoke badly of any of them. Whereas another teacher would say, "Oh God, this one is horrible and that one is horrible." The only things I heard her say were positive, and she meant them.

Dr. Hora: Extremely important. Every time we criticize someone and complain about someone, we are hurting ourselves. If we point one finger at someone there are three other fingers pointing toward us. Do you have the impression that you are being told to be optimistic? Cockeyed optimists? No, we are not talking about being optimistic. What are we talking about?

Student: Seeing life through God.

Dr. Hora: Yes, being enlightened by knowing reality. Reality is all good. God has created a perfect universe, and in divine reality there is no evil, no sickness, no suffering. Everything everywhere is already all right. So you don't have to be optimistic and you don't have to be pessimistic. You just have to be in touch with reality.

Student: So, Dr. Hora, does that also mean that we don't have to keep ourselves from complaining?

Dr. Hora: There is no law against keeping yourself from complaining, but if you do that you are just a goody-two-shoes ...right? But it's not enough to refrain from complaining, because you will turn sour...right? You are not a cucumber. (laughter) We are not talking about behavior. We are talking about understanding what is. Is you is or is you ain't?

Student: At work there is a lot of pressure. Everyone is pressured to do more for less. I go to work peaceful. And all of a sudden the pressure begins, and all I can see is that I fall into the trap. I resist it. My boss comes back from vacation. The work is getting done; we're working hard. He knows we need more help, but he has this irresistible urge to tell us how wonderful he is and how he wants more work done. I sit there saying, "I can't take it anymore. We need help. Everything is getting done." I know I am attacking it from the behavioral aspect, because I do not want to be subjected to his tirade of pressure. But I lose sight of God in this. I react and I want to let him have it.

Dr. Hora: You do let him have it.

Student: So I'm just attacking the behavior. I don't know what the right thoughts are. I mean, there seems to be a pressure to do more for less and it is never enough. So, I want to scream sometimes. I don't see God in that. There's just a lot of pressure. I want to complain, but I can't. (laughter)

Dr. Hora: We must admit that she's succeeded. (laughter) So what's the answer to this problem? We all know what pressure is. It is something that seems to be, but it isn't. And who is this individual who is being pressured?

Student: We pressure ourselves.

Dr. Hora: Now the Bible says that you are a non-dimensional transparency, a beam of light in divine consciousness. Have you ever tried to pressure a beam of light? What happens? What would happen to this student if she went to work with the clear awareness that she is a beam of light, and here comes the boss who is trying to pressure her?

Student: I laugh now, but I know I am just reframing myself from complaining.

Dr. Hora: Reframing? You ought to be in pictures. (laughter) The more substantial we believe that we are, the more vulnerable to pressure we become in our experience. That is why it is so dangerous to take ourselves seriously. A serious individual sees himself as very substantial — three dimensional, perhaps even four dimensional and heavy. The more we think of ourselves as substantial people, the more sensitive we are to being pressured. So put on a chiffon dress and ballet shoes and see yourself as a transparency for God, totally non-dimensional intelligence, pure intelligence and love...and you will see that nobody will be able to pressure you. And your presence will be appreciated.

Student: Especially in that chiffon dress. (laughter)

Dr. Hora: Actually we see that people suffer from each other's pressures to the extent that they think of themselves as substantial persons. The more substantial you are, the more susceptible to pressure you are. And when such people come around, the atmosphere becomes intolerable and heavy. It is just a thought. The idea of being pressured is a thought. It is interesting that in the movies, the heavies are the ones with the black hats, the mafia, the heavy guys. In Quakerism they have a term: a weighty friend. Who were the weighty friends? The senior members of a Quaker group are the weighty ones. Again, it is a disastrous concept. You are carrying a lot of weight. And if you think of yourself that way, in an office, if you are important and you have achieved a certain status and now you enjoy it, you begin to see yourself as a heavy. You have a command presence, and you do good work, and you delegate and the spirit of heaviness descends upon the corporation. It becomes corpulent, and then there is a lousy experience of depression. It's all mental.

Jesus was in a synagogue preaching and he said unflattering things there. They got very angry with him. They surrounded him and had the idea of grabbing him and taking him to a cliff and throwing him down the cliff, because that was how they saw him. But he knew that he was not a heavy. He was a lightweight, even lighter than Dan Quayle. They spoke of him as a lightweight. And so they couldn't see him, they couldn't pressure him, and they couldn't grab hold of him. They couldn't touch him. He had an idea that was different from their idea.

When your idea is different from other people's idea, they don't see you. The black people frequently complain that the whites cannot see them. Senior citizens complain that the young folk don't see them. People just see what they are pre-pared to see. And we experience what we are prepared to experience. But if we consistently understand the truth of our being, then we see that we are non-dimensional, incorporeal, spiritual transparencies for God. And then nobody will see us, but we'll be there and the work will be done, effortlessly, ef-fectively and efficiently. So it's good to know these things. It's interesting that normal people always want to carry a lot of weight, to be important in the eyes of others, and eat a lot. But on the path to enlightenment we have a longing to be trans-parent, peaceful, joyous, happy, and intelligent, accomplishing whatever needs to be accomplished, effortlessly.

Student: We hear this expression a lot, that a person has a lot of baggage, emotional baggage. So it can be true.

Student: So, if I see myself in a different context, does that mean that the experience will be different? Then there will be no pressure?

Dr. Hora: Absolutely. Guaranteed. You go visiting your parents and your sister, and sometimes it's okay, and you don't even catch cold. But sometimes you go there and everything goes wrong and it's miserable. It's the same food, the same dining room, the same kids, the same people. How do you explain it? What does our experience depend on?

Student: On our thoughts.

Dr. Hora: Yes. Sometimes we forget and go visiting in the disguise of being an important person who should be loved and admired and catered to. It's a disguise we put on when we go visiting. But sometimes we are in a sane condition, and we go visiting knowing the truth, that we are nothing, and it is a beautiful experience. The same goes for working in the office . . . right? So, it is important to know who we really are. The Texans . . . know. What do they know?

Student: "You is what you ain't." (laughter)

Dr. Hora: (laughter) The Texans say "You ain't never was nothin." Now we have a new definition of sanity. Sanity is knowing what we really are. And insanity is thinking that we are something else. How many times do people say to us, "You are somethin' else." Nothing comes into experience uninvited. (Seventh Principle) Many people have trouble with this principle. They say, "Are you trying to tell me that it's my fault that I've had a bad experience?" What would you say?

Student: It's not you, the individual. It's the thoughts.

Dr. Hora: It's the thoughts. Right. Nobody is being blamed for nothin'. It is the thoughts that prevail in consciousness that determine our experiences. Sometimes they can be fantastic.

Student: We don't create the thoughts, do we? Don't thoughts just come to us?

Dr. Hora: Yes, we are victims of thoughts from the sea of mental garbage. Once I knew a man who always wanted to be a big wheel in business. He was driving on the New Jersey turnpike, and as he was driving on the turnpike, a truck was coming from the other side of the road. A big wheel fell off the truck and rolled over the barrier into his lane and hit his car in the front windshield. Now, isn't that fantastic? What a strange accident! You see, sometimes we ask for it. Whatever we are thinking about can be asking for trouble. How did that truck driver know what to do? You see, there are no accidents. There are only thoughts manifesting themselves as experiences, from the trivial to the tragic, or anything in between.

Student: The truck driver needed to have some thoughts also...

Dr. Hora: Yes, he was thinking about his girl friend, and what he will do tonight in the motel. What do truck drivers think about? Mostly beer, or something like that. Anyway, we are learning to think right. What is right thought?

Student: God-centered.

Dr. Hora: God-centered, right. The Truth of Being, the right understanding of the Truth of Being abolishes all invalid thoughts and gives us immunity and protection. That's why the Bible says, "Because thou hast made the Lord . . . thy habitation, there shall no evil befall thee, neither shall any plague come nigh thy dwelling" (Psalms 91:9–10). So safety in every area of life depends on learning to monitor our thoughts continuously, and knowing which thoughts are valid and which thoughts are not valid.

Student: Dr. Hora, you were talking earlier about the economy and the nature of the contagion that takes place when people start thinking about how bad things are. And it grows and grows. But when we read in the newspaper that thousands of stores are closing and hundreds of thousands of people are losing their jobs . . . and it is true that this is happening . . . what is the valid way to look at this? Are these people victims of their own erroneous thoughts?

Dr. Hora: Yes, of course.

Student: And that's not negative thinking?

Dr. Hora: Not even George Bush is to be blamed for it. The tendency is to blame. It is basic human nature to seek self-confirmatory experiences.

Student: But what about people who have been working for 20 to 25 years, who never wanted not to have a job and have put in honest, hard work and effort all those years and are suddenly out of a job? It seems hard to understand that after all these years they decided they didn't want to work anymore, or they suddenly have an ignorant thought.

Dr. Hora: Well, we have spoken of the secret of contagion. What makes problems contagious? It is not only syphilis that is contagious and AIDS and diseases of all kinds, but also economic diseases. We now have computer sicknesses; did you know that sometimes there is an epidemic of computer diseases? They call it a virus. What is this? It is just collective, negative, self-confirmatory thinking. It is the curse of mankind. It is inevitable, but not necessary. The Bible says, "A thousand shall fall at thy side and ten thousand on thy right hand, but it shall not come nigh thee" (Psalms 91:7). "For he shall give his angels charge of thee, to keep thee in all thy ways" (Psalms 91:11). What does that mean?

Student: I guess it means that if we are mindful of God this will protect us from the contagion of negative thinking and self-confirmatory thinking.

Dr. Hora: Thousands are losing their jobs, living on the streets, losing their homes, are sick and suffering. Hundreds and thousands are dying of AIDS. It is very dismal looking, but it is all just another form of international self-confirmatory ideation, which people are eager to pick up. "No evil shall befall thee, neither shall any plague come nigh thy dwelling" (Psalms 91:10). It is possible to be immune to the afflictions of the human race provided we understand the message of the 91st psalm. Have you ever heard of the 91st psalm? The greatest gift of God to mankind is the 91st psalm. It is life-saving.

Student: Do individuals have a proclivity toward certain types of invalid thinking?

Dr. Hora: Yes, we have a great variety of choices available.

Student: But I tend to catch myself, continually, on the same track, more or less.

Dr. Hora: Not enough originality. (laughter)

Student: Okay. (laughter)

Student: Is that what you mean by a mode of being in the world?

Dr. Hora: That's right, sure.

Student: What amazes me is that when you clarify the issues, it is easy to see that what you are saying is true and valid. But when confirmation hits, it's as if we become completely blind. When that takes over, we are blind. We don't really see anything.

Dr. Hora: How can something that is nothing take over?

Student: It seems that way. It seems like it has a life of its own. When we are in that life it's hard to see anything else.

Dr. Hora: Well, we are here now, and we are studying and seeking to understand that we are not in that life.

Student: But what scares me is that the life could be turned off so quickly, with the tendency to slip into darkness. It amazes me how that can happen.

Dr. Hora: "And this is the condemnation, that light has come into the world and men loved darkness rather than light, because their deeds were evil" (John 3:19). Yes, unfortunately, we are all prone to this. We must be alert and on guard and understand that, just because millions of people are suffering and vulnerable, we don't have to be. Now Jesus had a way of describing it beautifully. He said, "Broad is the way and wide is the gate which leadeth to destruction, and many there are who enter therein; but narrow is the gate and straight is the road that leadeth to Metapsychiatry...* and few there are who find it" (Matthew 7:13–14). Isn't that fantastic? He sure knew his stuff. (laughter)

Student: Aside from coming here, we can easily fall into or convince ourselves that what is invalid is really valid. Is there anything else you can recommend to help us with this?

Dr. Hora: Well, the great danger is the habit of conformity. We conform to prevailing opinions and what seems to be. If somebody settles down in Greenwich Village, there is a great tendency to conform to the prevailing modes of life styles, and one can easily become a gay, a homosexual. You don't have to go to school to learn this. You just pick it up. It's easy. They, the experts, are always trying to find some biological basis for homosexuality. Nonsense. It is the value system express-ing itself in certain types of behavior. "God has created man [perfect, in his own image and likeness],** but they sought out many inventions" (Ecclesiastes 7:29). You don't have to be so invented. We can stick with the truth.

---

*"life"
**And God said, "let us make man in our image, after our likeness..." (Genesis 1:26).

3

Freedom and Corruptibility

Student: I would like to ask about freedom. I don't really know what to ask except when we understand the meaning of things, of thoughts, that helps us to see what stands in the way of our freedom, right? Understanding the meaning? But if we understand the meaning of something and it doesn't manifest itself in freedom, then what's the problem? (laughter). I don't really know what question to ask. I just want to know how to be free.

Dr. Hora: You could ask, "What is freedom?" (laughter) It is a philosophical and a political question. What is it? What is freedom? Who knows?

Student: What comes to mind, because I also cry for freedom, is to live a life in spontaneity, with no self-concern, to be free of fears and wants, to live a life of spontaneity.

Student: You said in the past that freedom is knowing the truth.

Dr. Hora: Exactly. That's what I said. Guilty as charged. (laughter) Freedom is knowing the truth. Isn't that an interesting definition? Who would have suspected it? The student described freedom as being within the context of action. But freedom is not an activity. Freedom is a condition of existence. It's a quality of existence. Jesus knew the difference between going on a boat or doing this or that and that's not freedom. No other philosopher has ever formulated freedom in this way. He said freedom is knowing the truth. "Ye shall know the truth, and the truth shall make you free" (John 8:32). When I first heard it, it blew my mind, as the saying goes. Freedom is knowing the truth. It's a fantastic leap of consciousness. I read all these philosophers, and nobody defines freedom this way. Once you understand this, you become free. The right understanding of the definition of freedom sets you free. Isn't that fantastic? If you know the truth, you are free. How is that?

Student: There is nothing that can hurt you if you know the truth.

Dr. Hora: We like this definition that Jesus offered of freedom, but how would we define un-freedom? What is the opposite of freedom?

Student: Slavery. Mental slavery.

Student: Not knowing the truth. (laughter)

Student: Self-confirmation.

Dr. Hora: Well, certainly these are part of the picture. But actually the opposite of freedom is ignorance. People are not free because they are ignorant. They don't know the truth, and they are enslaved by their misconceptions of life. Jesus' definition of freedom as knowing the truth shows us that freedom's

opposite consists of not knowing the truth, which is being ignorant. And we know that when we are ignorant we bring
all kinds of misery into the world and upon ourselves. Everything revolves around the central issue of existence; from the
Christly perspective either you are free or you are ignorant.
So there you have it. Blessed are the ignorant for they will
be miserable and blame other people. (laughter) Freedom is a
central issue of life. In Metapsychiatry all our studies revolve
around the issue of freedom, of knowing, of understanding
what freedom is. "You shall know the truth and the truth shall
make you free" (John 8:32). If this definition means something to you, you will never blame anything on anybody else.
When people have problems, they always start out by asking,
"Who is to blame? Who did it? Why?" They want to find out
who to blame. But if you know the definition of truth, you
never blame anybody. You will just say, "Well, I need to get
acquainted with the Truth of Being." You know that we define ceaseless prayer as the sincere contemplation of the Truth
of Being. Through contemplation, we discover what freedom
is . . . contemplative meditation. The Buddha spent all his life
contemplating the truth, and he realized freedom.

Student: It's not enough to know the meaning of our problems.
I mean the meaning is always some form of ignorance, but we
need, I guess, to work with the second intelligent question to
come to know the truth.

Dr. Hora: What is the second intelligent question? Who did it?
(laughter) Who's to blame? How much does it cost? (laughter)
   What does knowing the truth do? When we think about
freedom, we immediately want to think in terms of "Somebody has to do something," or "Somebody has to stop doing

something." Right? In reality nobody can do anything. Under-standing freedom is not an activity, and this is very difficult for most people to realize. By learning to do something, you are not gaining freedom and you are not gaining the truth. What enters into the situation when we desire to know the truth? What can you do to know the truth?

Today I spoke to a man who has spent years and years of study and reading to find out what he has to do in order to be free. He cannot imagine that there is something in life, in human experience where nothing can be done. What do you do to know the truth? What do you do? Exercises?

Student: It's a tough question, when you really think about it. Obviously with me, I am still on the wrong track because I really don't understand it.

Dr. Hora: Yes, you are operational about the truth.

Student: You say that we need to be sincerely interested. I seem to hear that is an operational issue and yet I don't think that being sincerely interested is operational.

Dr. Hora: Of course.

Student: But yet I seem to see it that way. It's very frustrating.

Dr. Hora: How do you do the interest?

Student: I would like to have my mind blown. I would like to —

Dr. Hora: Just contemplate the fact that you cannot kick anybody in the behind; you cannot do anything; you cannot scratch yourself. There is no way that you can find an activity which will help you to understand the truth and become free.

What can give it to us? It's a mind boggling thing that people who study Metapsychiatry go through hell trying to figure out how to be free and how to know the truth. It cannot be figured out and you cannot do anything. I remember years ago people were very upset because I told them understanding cannot be done. Nobody can do it. It was unacceptable to this audience because they were mostly physicians, and they are activists, and operationalists. That is why they operate. (laughter) You cannot do it. But a sincere interest in considering the issue will make it happen. Understanding cannot be done. Understanding comes by the grace of God when the interest is sincere.

Student: We can't manufacture the interest either.

Dr. Hora: Exactly.

Student: So what's a student to do?

Dr. Hora: These are the positive values of suffering. Suffering can help us to understand the truth that sets us free.

Student: Would that be — for example, in the Bible when Jesus was always saying, "I am the truth," are we then to aspire to that Christ consciousness? I am that quality?

Dr. Hora: He was saying the truth is existential. It's a quality of enlightened life, and we are that truth that we seek.

Student: When you say that, what comes to mind is that you said we have to see ourselves as qualities. Would that help, rather than seeing ourselves as persons?

Dr. Hora: Yes, absolutely.

Student: That's freedom.

Dr. Hora: Jesus said that he is the way, the truth, and the life (John 14:6) and by him any man passing into this truth will find pasture and he will really know what life is. It is qualitative, not operational or quantitative. It's just a quality of consciousness that leads us to peace, assurance, gratitude, love and ha, ha. (laughter)

Student: John the Baptist said "Prepare ye the way" (Matthew 3:3). It seems to me that somehow we have to do something to prepare.

Dr. Hora: When we are sincerely contemplating the Truth of Being, we are preparing ourselves for the discovery of Christhood, which we cannot do. But by the sincerity of our interest, it happens. How many times do we read in the papers about inexplicable healings that take place in some people's lives? They are called miracles, but it is just that when we discover the nature of truth, our whole viewpoint on reality changes.

Student: Can you help me see contemplation as a non-action or as not an activity?

Dr. Hora: Yes. It is not something we do; it is something we focus attention on, and it does set us free. The most remarkable thing about enlightenment is that it is action which is non-action; but it is happening. We cannot make it happen and we cannot repeat it either. It comes upon us when we see that this is it. I heard that a little three-year boy was getting up in the morning and he said to his mother, "Today I am going to eat waffles and we shall have no arguments about it." (laughter)

Okay, you started all these troubles. (laughter) Now tell us, what do you get out of contemplating freedom? I think that is what you were aiming at. How can you be free from your mother? (laughter)

Student: Free from my mother's thoughts.

Dr. Hora: Right. Most people are encumbered with mother — mother fixation. In European psychological and philosophical literature, it's always mother who robs us of our freedom.

Student: How is that not blaming?

Dr. Hora: That IS blaming. I am not defending it. I am just reminding you.

Student: You say that your mother's thoughts are making you a prisoner.

Dr. Hora: She doesn't really. We accept the fantasy that she has the power to cause us problems.

Student: It's not real. So then you have to transcend that thought, because, while you have that thought, you are blaming.

Dr. Hora: Right. No one is to blame.

Student: So you are not free if you are blaming someone.

Dr. Hora: Yes, of course.

Student: So you are not going to do anything about your mother's thoughts. You are not going to say, "Well, I have to not pay any attention to my mother's thoughts," or something like that. You just transcend the idea that your mother's thoughts are hurting you. So then you are free.

Dr. Hora: Yes.

Student: I actually have an example of that. I called my mother to wish her a happy birthday. She hasn't been feeling well and my father answered and he said, "Oh, I am so glad you called; you can give her a reason to live." I said to myself, "No, thank you." I said, "No, I am not God. There is only one God and he is responsible for her, not me." To myself. (laughter) When I would speak to her I wouldn't be filled with guilt that I wasn't living up to her expectations. I can't be the reason for her to live. That is a misconception and has nothing to do with me. We spoke, there was laughter, and I hung up the phone and I was free. I wasn't obligated to anything at that point other than to acknowledge that God is her life, not me. It had nothing to do with me. All I could do was be as loving as I can under the circumstances as they come up, because sometimes it's not that easy and sometimes it's easy. It was liberating and I didn't have to accept what was being thrown at me. That was such a relief. I was joyous for the rest of the day. Little by little. I guess every experience is an opportunity to acknowledge what we learn here and to practice it.

Dr. Hora: No rabbi ever spoke like that.

Student: So in this life, we only get glimpses of freedom? It's not always available. We keep making these same mistakes over again. When we are healed of the fears, then we are free.

Dr. Hora: When it comes to these issues, you can only speak about yourself. You have a carte blanche to speak about this. (laughter) We can only set ourselves free. Nobody can really relieve you of the guilt that mother has thrown at you. You have to understand your life.

Student: It's easy to see how we are prisoners of all these fears and thoughts. When we are relieved of the fears, we are healed of the fears and we are free.

Dr. Hora: We are healed of wanting somebody to carry the burden of our sense of guilt. The children feel guilty, the parents feel guilty, Mrs. Calabash feels guilty. (laughter)

Student: Wherever she is. (laughter)

Student: I remember you saying that guilt was bragging.

Dr. Hora: Guilty as charged.

Student: When guilt is felt, and the thought comes that I am bragging and that I think I am so important that I can be influencing others, then I can know that I am bragging about how powerful I am. The guilt disappears now because I always remember that guilt is bragging.

Student: So compassion does not carry with it the idea of fixing someone. I guess when I think of my mother who has just been visiting, it's hard to see her suffering. It's hard to see her elderly and suffering and anxious, and I guess the guilt would come because there is not much that I can do about it. I try and then it doesn't work. Then I can be compassionate, but I have to get rid of the idea of fixing, or helping, or changing or alleviating. That's hard.

Dr. Hora: If you have a better idea, we would be willing to consider it. (laughter)

Student: Does it work the same way, that knowing the truth would heal all those thoughts?

Dr. Hora: Knowing the Truth of Being will set you free.

Student: Thoughts of trying to help or make things better, or feeling sorry, would all be eliminated?

Dr. Hora: We could say it removes the interaction ruminations of someone who has been enslaved into guilt.

Student: When you say this comes from the grace of God. What does that really mean?

Dr. Hora: Did I say that?

Student: Yes, many times I have heard you say — Once I said, "How is it that I am here studying and learning?" And you said, "Through the grace of God, don't question it. (laughter) Be grateful." But I don't really know what that means, the grace of God.

Dr. Hora: Well, God is a cosmic intelligence, a creative force that is essentially benevolent. Now if you are aware of such a force, you could say like they say in the movies, "The force is with you." (laughter) So we accept this wonderful blessing and just call God's grace our self-sufficiency in all things. Suppose somebody would ask you, "What is God and who is he, and how can we know him? How old is he?" Now we can say it is a cosmic power which is benevolent. A lady stopped me on 72nd Street yesterday and she said, "You have such a benevolent face. Where do you come from?" (laughter) And

I said in a very kindly way, "Lady, what business is that of yours?" (laughter) That was the end of the conversation.

Student: You know, that's a very good example of something, because in that statement, saying "Lady, what business is that of yours," it is very obvious that there is a sense of not owing her anything, and I realize that I feel like I owe everybody something. There is some catch. What is the meaning of that?

Dr. Hora: You lose your freedom right away if you allow somebody to flatter you. We cannot accept flattery because it is corrupting. Do you realize you have been corrupted in your life by mother's love?

Student: If you had felt that if you did not answer politely and this lady will not like you, then you are immediately corrupted.

Dr. Hora: You have lost your sense of freedom.

Student: In a situation like that, does it help in consciousness to recognize that any real goodness actually is really divine? Is that good for us to know that?

Dr. Hora: Yes. Some people called Jesus "good master" and he refused to accept it. He said, don't call me good. Only God is good. "Why callest thou me good? There is none good but one, that is, God" (Matthew 19:17). He didn't accept flatteries.

Student: So in a way, inside we can be grateful. I mean the positive part of it is that if there is goodness, then that is God. We don't have to take it personally.

Dr. Hora: Yes.

Student: When you were speaking about the older mother, we look upon her with compassion, but we don't look to fix or do something. There is this phenomenon of old age and there is this phenomenon of suffering and a lot of it seems to exist on this planet. How is one to look through that? I know you say we don't say, "I don't care," —

Dr. Hora: Compassion must not be confused with pity.

Student: It seems hard not to at times, because when there is some real form of suffering and it presents itself to you all the time, how do you remain above it? I know you need to overcome the world, but it's staring at you all the time, this situation.

Dr. Hora: Who is staring?

Student: I meant that the situation is present, of the sick people.

Dr. Hora: You are only staring at beautiful women. (laughter)

Student: Maybe this is where I am personalizing things, because I might say that it's their dream, it's their consciousness, but there seems to be this impulse to do something.

Dr. Hora: Like what?

Student: I mean to feel responsible to make them feel better, to perk them up. I know we can respond in a loving way, but it seems there is an impulse to do more.

Dr. Hora: You cannot love if you respond in the same tone with which you are being buttered up. That is not love; that's mutual bullshitting, which is socially considered very much desirable. It is called nice, being nice. All mothers are saying, "Be nice," ...right? It is not nice to be nice. It is nice to be forthright — forthright and benevolent and non-conditional. If you meet the Buddha on the road, what would you do?

Student: Slay him.

Student: Tell him to mind his own business. (laughter)

Dr. Hora: Is this nice, to slay the Buddha? What does this Zen story mean?

Student: It's exactly the story that you told about the encounter with the woman. She might have been saying, "Here's Buddha." I mean she might have seen you as embodying it somehow, and you slayed her.

Dr. Hora: The Buddha is not a person. The Christ is not a rabbi. It is a quality. The Buddha is a quality of incorruptibility. The Bible says, "So when this corruptible shall have put on incorruption, and this mortal shall have put on immortality, then shall be brought to pass the saying that is written, Death is swallowed up in victory" (1 Corinthians 15:54). What did that mean?

Student: That only a person can die. If you know who you are, then maybe —

Dr. Hora: The corruptibility has to die. What was Paul talking about? Freedom from being corruptible and yielding to seductive flatteries brings you back your true identity, and you come alive. If you yield to seductive flatteries, you are dead, because you have yielded to this fiction or lack of identity just in order to be nice back to one who is nice to you, and together you go down the drain because both of you are lying.

Student: What's the harm? You're nice, they're nice, you pass and you go on?

Dr. Hora: Right. You didn't understand a word I was talking about in the past ten minutes.

Student: I don't appreciate the harm.

Dr. Hora: You are losing your sense of authenticity. Do you know this French word? You lose your sense of authenticity, if you yield to the seductiveness of flattery. It is insincere.

Student: Isn't it being civil? It's what people do. It's a routine; you don't take it seriously. They say good morning; you say good morning. There is no seriousness. You just move on; you pass each other and that's it.

Dr. Hora: Yes.

Student: What's the big deal? (laughter)

Dr. Hora: Right. Actually he talks like that, you know, but he is not like that. He is very outspoken in a brutal sort of way. (laughter) No, we are just reminded of this Biblical quotation which is rather startling if you consider it, because the presumption is that everybody is corrupt. The world is filled with corruptible and corrupt people. If you are corruptible and corrupt, what can you expect? Everybody is lying. How can you become a forthright, Christlike, enlightened individual, a man of the Word?

Student: By not taking it seriously. You do it and they do it. It's the way people interact, but you don't put any significance on it.

Dr. Hora: The Biblical quotation implies that if you are corruptible, you are dead.

Student: If you take it seriously. I mean if you take flattery or a person makes a compliment and you take it seriously, then you are corruptible. Some nice old lady says, "Good morning, it's nice to see you," and then you think, "I must be special because she is addressing me." Then you are taking it seriously. If she says, "Good morning," and you say, "Oh, good morning to you," then you move on. I don't think you would be corruptible; you are just being civil.

Dr. Hora: Where do you come from? Who is your mother? What is your job? How old are you? What kind of girls do you like? Have I got a girl for you. (laughter)

Student: That is intrusive.

Student: In the example, you used flattery as the error. But it could be intimidation just as well as flattery, couldn't it? I mean if you are intimidated, then you are corrupted. I mean there are various forms it could take. You happened to use the example of flattery but it could take other forms and it's really the same thing, isn't it?

Dr. Hora: We don't know the details. There are many ways that people manipulate each other's thoughts and motives that we don't know. It's just a little incident. I just took a stand against flattery. If I accept flattery, pretty soon I will go and stand in front of a mirror for an hour and that is not healthy.

There is a very cute advertisement on the television about a man who had a beautiful dog, a dalmatian, and he bought the dog Alpo because the ad said it makes the dog shiny and healthy looking. So he did buy this food and the dog gobbled it up and then ran in front of the mirror admiring himself. The owner said, "I have ruined this dog." (laughter)

Student: What is the difference between taking a stand against something invalid, like the example you gave, and being interactive? I just keep thinking about situations at work where there is a lot of intimidation. I see that all the time. I am just trying to think of how one can take a stand.

Dr. Hora: Take a stand and lose his job.

Student: Without losing his job. (laughter)

Dr. Hora: There are situations when wisdom bids you to keep your mouth shut. You don't have to answer to everybody who is trying to corrupt you. You just take notice.

Student: Well mentally, you may not say anything.

Dr. Hora: Right. Sure. No problem. But if you yield to flattery all day long, frequently you might begin to stand in front of the mirror like the dog, looking at yourself. I don't think there is vanity in dogs. I think we read it into dogs, but they don't really know that they are beautiful or something. Don't you think so? They don't have this weakness, the dogs. They only think about other dogs. Did Charlie say something when you came home? (laughter)

Student: I was just thinking that every time he comes back in the room, I am the one who says to him how beautiful you look. He gets all excited. I don't think he knows it.

Dr. Hora: You ruined the dog. (laughter)

Student: Mind your own business. (laughter)

4

Wanting to Be Right

Student: What about O. J.?

Dr. Hora: You would like to talk about O. J.?

Student: It seems that everyone is fascinated with this trial. I guess everyone stopped what they were doing so they could hear the verdict. Then there has been a lot of emotional outpouring one way or the other about the verdict. All along people have been, at the very least, interested. I am very interested in the trial. What could be the meaning of that fascination with the whole episode?

Dr. Hora: People would like to be lawyers. Everybody wants to be right. People are willing to kill each other just to be right... right? It's amazing how many legal experts there are. (laughter)

Student: So it's an intellectual exercise. You form an opinion and you think you are right, and then you look to someone to confirm the fact that you are right?

Dr. Hora: What is the meaning of the desire to be right?

Student: Self-confirmation.

Dr. Hora: That's right. You are right. (laughter) You know the story about the Rabbi? Are we coming here to learn to be right? Is that why you come here, so you could think of yourself as the one who is right?

Student: Based on last week's meeting, I think the true test is to demonstrate. Unless one reminds oneself, one can just stay on a superficial level and not seek transformation with this information. It's easy to be right and to know the principles. But then it seems as if there is this next step of transformation and to live according to it. Yet it seems easier just to be right, to know this information and be content that I got it. I think there is a hesitation to go further, or laziness.

Student: Do you mean that somebody would be coming here so that they would think that they are right? In what context? You mean compared with other people who don't come here?

Dr. Hora: People who don't come here, they are wrong. (laughter)

Student: That is a little bit of a problem because I think that anybody that doesn't come here doesn't know anything.

Dr. Hora: You are right. (laughter)

Student: That can't be right. If we had that attitude ...

Dr. Hora: What is ceaseless prayer?

Student: You have defined it as the sincere contemplation of the Truth of Being.

Dr. Hora: Did you say contemplation of the Truth of Being? Okay, so then we are not seeking to be right; we are seeking to know the Truth of Being. If we know the Truth of Being, will we be right? No. We will seek to know the Truth of Being. Nobody can be right. Only the truth can be right. No individual in the world can be right. If Galileo had wanted to be right, they almost burned him at the stake because he pronounced a certain idea that was true. But he didn't claim to be right. He claimed that there is this reality which manifests itself astronomically in a certain way. They wanted to kill him because they misunderstood that he was motivated to show that he was right. All the warfare and uprisings and conflicts in the world occur because man in his mental vanity has a desire to claim that he is right. Is the Pope right? Did you hear him say that he is right? No. He says the Church is right. Of course he is wrong. Walter Cronkite is right. (laughter) He says, "That's the way it is." Galileo eventually came to the point where he didn't claim anymore that he was right. There was a beautiful picture recently of Galileo and his struggle. So we are not seekers for right. We are seekers to discern the truth. We pray for the truth. We don't pray that we should be proven to be right.

Now what would happen if in American jurisprudence, in the justice system, people stopped looking to prove that they are right? There would be no argument. Nothing stands in the way of the truth. The truth is not personal; the truth Is. If we are interested in knowing the truth, then we are true seekers of the truth and there are no more problems. The television shows could close down and there would be nothing to talk about. All these experts would be silenced, and if nobody knew the truth, it's all right too, as long as people admit that they don't know. Nobody wants to admit that he doesn't know. Everybody has opinions. Have you heard some people spouting opinions? "In my opinion" — everybody wants to spout his opinion. What are you saying when you say, "In my opinion?" When you say, "In my opinion," you are claiming personal knowledge — "I am right. I know." The claim of personal knowledge is a lie. There is no such thing.

Student: What does it mean when you are irritated when somebody states his or her opinion so definitely, and you know that there is no such thing as an opinion, and yet here it is?

Dr. Hora: Do you really know that?

Student: I guess I don't; otherwise, I wouldn't be... Am I reacting?

Dr. Hora: You are reacting, of course, because everybody is irritated by the knowledgeableness of everybody else.

Student: The claim of the knowledgeableness?

Dr. Hora: Yes. Are you claiming this? Divine Mind alone is the intelligence that knows the truth. We are not Divine Mind. We are controlled by Divine Mind. If people understand that the issue is knowing the truth, there would be no arguments. There would be no discord. There would be no wars. There would be no rumors of wars and there would be no self-righteousness. Self-righteousness you will find in all these discussions. It is intellectual self-confirmatory ideation. I know. So I have to deprive you of these pleasures of contentiously fighting for acknowledgement of personal knowledge. We don't have that. There is no such thing. You know the story about the Rabbi. Does everybody know the story about the Rabbi? Shall I tell you? You won't be bored?

There was this Rabbi who was in charge of a congregation and there were some members of that congregation who argued about some issue and each one claimed to be right. They asked the Rabbi to arbitrate. Who is right? The Rabbi said, "First I will listen to one and then I will listen to the other and I will tell you who is right." So the first one told his story and the Rabbi said, "I can see your point; you are really right." Then the other guy came and he told his story, and the Rabbi thought about it and then he said, "I can see you are right." And his wife Sarah was standing by listening to him and she said to the Rabbi, "Listen Rabbi, you say that this one is right and that one is right. This cannot be right." The Rabbi thought and thought and thought and tried to understand. After a while he came to say, "Yes, I know. You know what Sarah? You are right too." (laughter) Everybody wants to be right. It's a dead issue.

Student: When it says, "Agree with thine adversary..."

Dr. Hora: That's bad advice.

Student: I am not sure I know the whole passage.

Dr. Hora: What did Jesus mean by saying, "Agree with thine adversary quickly whiles thou art in the way with him"? (Matthew 5:25).

Student: Not to argue or to try to be right. Drop the situation. Focus on the truth.

Dr. Hora: That's right. Neither to agree nor disagree. Is that possible?

Student: It's really possible; but as you said before, we just have to practice it all the time and always be aware. It seems that every step of the way there is always something to distract us or to engage us or something to get involved in . . . opinions.

Dr. Hora: Only if you are not a student of Metapsychiatry, for then you are a hopeless case.

Student: Sometimes stating an opinion seems so innocent. It doesn't seem like it's such a terrible thing. Yet based on what you are saying, is it never appropriate to give an opinion?

Dr. Hora: Right. (laughter) You are right. It is a precious knowledge to understand that it is not valid to express or cherish or harbor or spout opinions. It is invalid and if you recognize it, you will not get yourself into trouble with people. Then you will neither agree nor disagree.

Student: You will then see it's an issue of people looking to be self-righteous?

Dr. Hora: If you spout opinions, yes.

Student: If you come across someone by yourself and you see that opinions are being put forth, if you neither agree nor disagree, you will tend to see that you are involved in a situation where people want to be self-righteous.

Dr. Hora: That's right. So you never join in the idiotic spouting. The lawyers were spouting opinions in the O. J. case, if you were watching television. Everybody had an opinion about who killed whom and why. Is he a black or is he Hispanic or is he a white man? If you are a white, then you know who killed whom. If you are Hispanic, you know that nobody's interested. (laughter) Everybody wants to be right, and this is a big issue. It is serious and troublesome. But if you refuse to express an opinion, they will think one of two things: they will think you are stupid or that you are hiding something.

Student: If you didn't find yourself saying, "I see that this is a situation where people are looking to be self-righteous," then you sort of back off. It seems to me you kind of withdraw from the situation.

Dr. Hora: They start pressuring you. You have to answer, "What's your opinion?"

Student: Once you spot that it's an erroneous exchange, what comes after that?

Dr. Hora: Silence.

Student: There must be something there to decide what's right.

Dr. Hora: In the silence there is the whisper of infinite mind.

Student: So you wait for a thought to occur?

Dr. Hora: You don't have to wait. It's right there. It is not necessary to have opinions. It is actually stupid. All wisdom is inherent in the Divine Mind and the Divine Mind doesn't fiddle around with opinions. It just Is and you let it be. What do you say when there is nothing to say?

Student: Good question. (laughter)

Student: Can you say I understand your point? Can you say you are entitled to your opinion? I value your opinion?

Dr. Hora: If you have no opinion, they explode with hatred. This is the human condition. It is frustrating to them, and they don't believe it. If you say to somebody, "I have no opinions," they will not believe it.

Student: If we sincerely understand that the individual is entitled to whatever he or she might think about the situation, does that help? If we really, really know in our heart, does it help the situation?

Dr. Hora: No. (laughter) The only right thing would be to say, "I cherish no opinions. I am a truth seeker. I seek to know the truth. Opinions will not help me in that direction." Then they will say you are just a dumbbell. You have to accept that. There is no use arguing.

Student: A lot of time, they just don't notice. They are too busy talking about their own opinions.

Dr. Hora: There is a scene described in Job where he is arguing with God and the devil and they cannot get to first base. And he suddenly puts his hand on his mouth and shuts up and stops entering into the disputes and opinions of who is right. Is the devil right? Is God right? Is Job right? He shut up and indicated that there are no opinions to speak about and afterwards he exclaimed, "I have known thee by the hearing of the ear but now my eye seeth thee" (Job 42:5). What does it mean that my eye seeth thee? Who is this thee? It's God; it's the truth. We reach a point where we realize that there is no such thing as being right or wrong. The truth is part of divine reality. It is what really is. As they say, "Is you is or is you ain't?" And then there is no more arguing and no more frustration. The truth is. To express opinions is a lie.

Student: If Job understood the truth, then . . .

Dr. Hora: He put his hand on his mouth, which is sign language indicating that I am not going to enter in this discussion. When you shut up, then the truth may dawn on you.

Student: Then you can say something.

Dr. Hora: No. (laughter)

Student: Suppose you are in a business meeting or something like that and trying to decide a course of action or something and there are opinions on all sides. So there is an individual there who is quiet and there is a moment of grace where he or she understands . . .

Dr. Hora: One can break out of this impasse, and, with the grace of God, Divine Mind inspires them not to try to spout opinions, and the whole thing drops out and then a new issue has to emerge.

Student: It seems that the truth has nothing to do with the situation that the individuals are arguing about.

Dr. Hora: Of course not. (laughter) It's frustrating . . . right?

Student: It's hard to understand. I thought the truth would break the deadlock so to speak.

Dr. Hora: It does. When you shut up.

Student: But it's of no benefit to anyone except the individual.

Dr. Hora: Everybody benefits from that silence. It reveals itself, clears itself.

Student: In a situation where an individual is silent and allows for ideas to flow or somehow the debate stops, then the right idea can come. It still seems that in the business setting you are there with an objective. You are there to be useful. So one way to be useful would be ...

Dr. Hora: No, you are not there to be useful. You are there to be right. (laughter) What does the Zen Master do when the student insists that he answer him?

Student: He hits them. (laughter)

Dr. Hora: Well, you know you have had that experience. (laughter)

Student: It seems to me that if we really understood what you are saying tonight, about no opinions, not being right, that would be total freedom. We wouldn't be involved in judgments, being critical or any of those things. We would truly be free.

Dr. Hora: Sure. How many people suffer serious illness because they are loaded with critical thoughts and they were advised not to express them? If you are loaded with critical thoughts and you squelch them, you get sick ... right?

Somewhere I wrote a poem about this, some years ago. Do you know this poem? It dealt with this issue. A few years ago it was published.

Student: It may be on the jacket of the booklet. There were some poems at the end of one of our booklets.

Dr. Hora: I will have to write some new books and they will turn out to be old books. (laughter)

Student: In picking up tapes from years ago, I can see that the truth is the truth. Somehow I never heard that. (laughter)

Dr. Hora: It isn't aging. It's ageless.

Student: If we see that someone is suffering from being critical, and they are physically ill as a result of it, we can see the suffering and we can see the meaning and yet we cannot afford to make a judgment. It is easy to judge someone for that kind of ignorance. So...

Dr. Hora: So what's a mother to do?

Student: How can you give people any kind of comfort when they don't want to hear the truth? They are stuck with their way of thinking, yet they look to you for some comfort even though they are really not interested.

Dr. Hora: Just throw in the towel. That's all.

Student: I guess we have to know the truth for ourselves. That's all we can ever do.

Dr. Hora: It's a funny thing about this wanting to help. It can make it worse. If somebody has a problem of being judgmental and it is eating him up inside, and he develops all kinds of symptoms that go from bad to worse, there is nothing you can do because he wouldn't listen.

Student: So you just observe that as a phenomenon. I guess we can't be afraid of it. We just have to see it for what it is. If we are not healed of our problems, if we don't understand our meanings, then it just takes over. It has to go somewhere. So it's something for which we could be grateful — that at least we understand the meaning — and we are not frightened by it. Just let it go at that.

Student: We talked about a similar thing in a private session in which I mentioned that I had a symptom and someone else had a symptom. You indicated they were both the result of critical thinking, and when I realized that that's all it was, it somehow relieved me totally because I no longer had to fear it. It was just a thought. The funny thing is my symptom went away and the other guy hasn't said a word about his either. I don't want to bring it up. (laughter)

Dr. Hora: You cannot bring it up.

Student: Because then he'll think about it and it will start all over again. He was talking about it constantly, but since the session he hasn't said a word about it. The issue is that the physical is mental and once that was clear, the fear disappeared, and I guess that's what allowed the symptom to appear.

Dr. Hora: It's like putting the hand on the mouth. It finishes the struggle, if you are sincere about it.

Student: One thing about when we are ruminating, we may not spout opinions to others but we constantly ruminate about ourselves. Is that the same thing?

Dr. Hora: Absolutely.

Student: So when we are ruminating, we are really saying, "I know better than God."

Dr. Hora: Sure. The husband I mentioned to you in Connecticut keeps nagging his wife. If only you would change.

He is not embarrassed about the stupidity of that statement. (laughter) He started out as a student of Metapsychiatry but very soon he dropped it because she wasn't changing. If only you would change. (laughter)

Student: Don't most people think that?

Dr. Hora: Sure.

Student: There are no opinions; there's no right or wrong. I have to hear it again. I mean it's mind boggling to think there is no opinion, no ruminating.

Dr. Hora: No criticizing.

Student: If you were really focused on the truth.

Dr. Hora: Right . . . there would be no struggle.

Student: I think the part that always seems to get me at work is the idea that I don't want to appear stupid. As long as I don't want to appear stupid, I always seem to have an opinion. If somebody comes and asks me . . .

Dr. Hora: Why don't you want to be stupid?

Student: Then they will say, "She doesn't belong in that job." (laughter)

Dr. Hora: It's good for you to be stupid.

Student: I don't get it from that perspective.

Dr. Hora: Then what is needed in changing the perspective? Getting away from the ideas which got us stuck, changing, talking about something irrelevant.

Student: If somebody comes to us...we have to understand we cannot afford to be right or wrong. We are not here to have an opinion. We are here to see if we can see the truth.

Dr. Hora: And shed light on the truth, which is rarely successful.

Student: I want to ask a direct question, a quantitative one, sort of.

Dr. Hora: Are you stupid or something? (laughter)

Student: Like 2 + 2 are four.

Dr. Hora: A mathematician told me it is more or less four.

Student: But if you are asked a direct question, isn't it appropriate to answer?

Dr. Hora: Seldom. (laughter)

Student: The only solution that I can see is to always make jokes, (laughter) because then people forget. You don't have to give an answer.

Dr. Hora: Sure. You're right.

Student: I think sometimes we get seduced into thinking the other person wants an answer or that they want an opinion or that they are really looking for something. A lot of the time they are not at all interested in what we might or might not have to say.

Dr. Hora: They want us to agree with them.

Student: That's true.

Dr. Hora: Isn't the human condition ridiculous?

Student: The more we see that it's ridiculous, the more important it seems to be interested in the truth. We can see how ridiculous and wearing it is. Every time I am aware that I got involved with something that is ridiculous, I am not apt to do it again. It seems helpful to see that. It's crazy, this idea of human goodness. People try to be good. I get annoyed. I can't stand it when somebody is good at my expense. (laughter) If someone is good, then someone has to be bad. How can we see that, when it occurs in a family context? If they are good, then obviously I am not and I find them very annoying. I know it's invalid. What's the right idea?

Dr. Hora: You just expressed it ... holding your mouth.

Student: So there again, it's an opinion. I am judging the individual. This is the way they deal with life and it's not my place to make a judgment. If I am interested in transcending self, then it doesn't matter whether I am good or bad. It's not the truth of my being. That's the issue. As long as I am taking it personally, then I am in trouble.

Dr. Hora: We are neither healthy nor sick, nor good nor bad. You are hardly anything.

Student: We are just stupid and we laugh all the time. (laughter)

Student: Remember you were talking a while back about competitiveness and how children are taught to be competitive from the earliest ages. The school system is sort of built on this, and what helped me was when you talked about a swimmer in the Olympics. Actually, the competition is to better their skill, to better their ability, to better the gifts they have been given, rather than to be better than someone else. That is more valid. I know that competitiveness is there, but what is the reason for trying to be better? When you get through the convoluted reasoning to see what's what, it seems to help. There seems to be good in being skilled and being efficient or whatever, but for what reason?

Student: I have a real problem with critical thinking with my sister-in-law in particular, because she drinks too much. So half the time she is passed out or something. You never know what you are going to find when you go up and talk to her.

Dr. Hora: Why is it your problem?

Student: Because I just know that's not the way to be.

Dr. Hora: Because you love her and you want to rescue her from alcoholism?

Student: It makes me angry that she is wasting her life and she is making it all a mess and she is making us do all these things for her.

Dr. Hora: So what is the meaning of being angry with that?

Student: It's really self.

Dr. Hora: She has a right to kill herself or drink herself into oblivion.

Student: Then we are the ones who have to take her to the hospital.

Dr. Hora: You can hire a taxi.

Student: What do I need to know to be free of those critical thoughts?

Dr. Hora: Well there is such a thing as a false sense of personal responsibility. If you are obsessed with that, you are going to suffer too.

Student: So there is no responsibility for her.

Dr. Hora: There is responsiveness where it is intelligent and manageable, but beyond that you are not your sister-in-law's keeper. You are your sister-in-law's sister-in-law. God didn't say to Abel, "You are your brother's keeper." Many religious people repeat this idea, that you are your brother's keeper. It doesn't say so in the Bible. What does it say?

Student: Are you your brother's keeper?

Dr. Hora: God asks this question: Are you your brother's keeper? ("Am I my brother's keeper?" Genesis 4:9) There is no answer. Nobody dared to answer because they were imbued with certain preconceived notions that we are obligated to be our brother's keeper, which is a self-confirmatory vanity. Who the hell are you? And if you try to rescue a drunk, that's what he will say: "Who the hell are you?" If we are asked nicely, we will help. But it's not an obligation. Neither is it a right. We have no right to stop somebody from drinking. We can take away his car key, but that's not a favor. That's just self-protection.

Student: So the idea also of being right is ... because I am thinking I am right and she is wrong for drinking. So that's an opinion.

Dr. Hora: A self-confirmatory opinion.

Student: How is it that AA works, because alcoholics, I understand, are helped in AA?

Dr. Hora: AA works only with people who have hit bottom. You know what that means.

Student: Shipwrecked.

Dr. Hora: Yes. Before they hit bottom, it doesn't work.

Student: The companion to that, Al Anon, helps let them hit bottom.

Dr. Hora: Nothing else will work. There has to be a certain ripening of misery.

Student: That's really true with most of us. We are unwilling to change until it becomes unbearable.

Dr. Hora: Right. Of course.

5

The Wisdom to Know the Difference

Student: I have no confidence that if I ask a question the answer will be forthcoming. Usually at work I'm not sure what answer will come, and I'm uneasy.

Dr. Hora: Could you give us an example?

Student: Well, today at lunch I noticed that I had a headache. I was alone and I asked the first intelligent question, "What is the meaning of my experience?" about the painful experience.

Dr. Hora: All right, good.

Student: I was not aware of a specific thing. I understand it must be an angry thought...

Dr. Hora: Yeah.

Student: But I'm not aware of an angry thought.

Dr. Hora: Does anybody know the angry thought that this student had at lunchtime, eating alone? (laughter) It's an open secret. (more laughter) I would like to ask you a question. The Bible says, "Discretion shall preserve thee, understanding shall save thee" (Proverbs 2:11). Metapsychiatry adds another line and says, "secretiveness will destroy thee." Now let me repeat, "Discretion shall preserve thee, understanding shall save thee, secretiveness will destroy thee." Who can explain this? It boils down to this: what is the difference between being discreet and being secretive?

Student: Well, it seems that with being discreet we are pondering and considering, but we are not holding anything back. We're not being secretive. We're being intelligent about what we are talking about when we're being discreet. And being secretive is kind of hiding.

Dr. Hora: That's true, but what is so destructive about secretiveness?

Student: It's dishonest, manipulative, and self-seeking.

Dr. Hora: Hmmm. What is so destructive about secretiveness?

Student: It's based on comparison thinking. The reason you are secretive is because you think you are going to get an A job rating if you keep the issue to yourself. And one would do that in order to be better than someone else, e.g., I'm better because I have this information.

Dr. Hora: You ain't hit it ... right?

Student: I'll give it a try. Secretiveness becomes a bed for fantasy, for if you are secretive you can weave thoughts in your own mind without your being exposed about what is going on. So we weave a fantasy.

Dr. Hora: It is important to understand the difference between secretiveness and discretion.

Student: It seems that secretiveness is repressing.

Dr. Hora: Repressing? So?

Student: Repression is harmful.

Student: In discretion there is an element of love, I think. In secretiveness, love is absent.

Dr. Hora: Now you're coming close. Okay, can somebody come even closer?

Student: Boasting. Secretiveness is a form of boasting.

Dr. Hora: How is that a form of boasting?

Student: It's a method of accomplishing or getting ahead in the world according to what you think is reality. But it's not that.

Student: Discretion is God-confirmatory while secretiveness is self-confirmatory.

Dr. Hora: You're close. That's right. Secretiveness is self-confirmatory; therefore, it is inevitably self-destructive. Everything that is self-confirmatory is also self-destructive. Look at the CIA; they have destroyed themselves completely — a secret service. (laughter) So, secretiveness is self-confirmatory. Discretion is considerate. When we are discreet we are protective of somebody else's comfort or safety or feelings; discretion is a positive quality that is protective of somebody else. Secretiveness is self-confirmatory.

Student: How is secretiveness self-confirmatory?

Dr. Hora: You are holding back something to protect yourself. When you are discreet, you are protecting somebody else, and that will preserve you. Isn't that interesting? Discretion will preserve you and secretiveness will destroy you.

Student: Sounds like discretion is the practice of compassion.

Dr. Hora: Correct. Absolutely. For instance, if you know that disclosing something about someone could be very embarrassing to that individual, you refrain from disclosing it and are being discreet by protecting another's interest and comfort. That's discretion and it will preserve you. Secretiveness that is protective of yourself will destroy you. Isn't that interesting? And understanding the difference will save you because you know the wisdom of knowing the difference. There is a tremendous difference and not many people give it a thought. Now when we are silent in the group, some of us are secretive and some of us are just discreet. Or maybe we just do not know the difference. Perhaps if we knew the difference there would be greater freedom of expression.

Student: When someone tells you a secret and you do not pass it on and you just keep it, is that being discreet?

Dr. Hora: That's right.

Student: Does this fit in? What is the difference between awareness and thinking? The reason I ask is because the further we are along in understanding, would we just be more aware and not thinking? It seems that it is easy to get caught in thought, whereas when awareness prevails it seems effortless.

Dr. Hora: Well, look here. We had a collective response to the student's question. Spontaneously, simultaneously, suddenly everybody knew, but he didn't. How is that possible?

Student: He gave us a hint? (laughter)

Dr. Hora: Anybody that has difficulty with meanings has the difficulty because he or she is inclined to want to figure it out. If you want to figure out the meaning of your experience you are being a thinker. You want to think about it and figure it out and that doesn't work. You have to be receptive and it will reveal itself to you spontaneously . . . just as it has revealed itself to the group, even though . . . he gave us a clue. But you all understood that very clearly. You see, the thinker has a hard time. Think about the thinker and suddenly you can see the tortured sculpture by Rodin. It tries to think. Thinking is very hard. It never gets us anywhere. But awareness is easy. The Buddha sits there. He is never thinking. He is spontaneously aware of whatever needs to be known. It comes to him from the Divine Mind.

Student: Is it important to have extensive knowledge of the ideas of Metapsychiatry before one is able to discern the meaning of a problem?

Dr. Hora: It is important to know the difference between thinking and awareness. That's it.

Student: I think once in group, it was suggested that when we're working with meanings that we reformulate the first intelligent question and say, "I would really like to know what the meaning is," and just asking it sincerely made it change somehow.

Dr. Hora: Yes, when you say that you are praying and you assume a humble, receptive attitude towards the meaning, then receptivity and humility are the doors which let in the meaning. Thinking is an arrogant position. The thinker wants to use his head to master the problem and all he gets is a worse headache. So it is not helpful to be a thinker. We're not anti-intellectuals; we have compassion for intellectuals, but they have a hard time. They use their heads but the head doesn't have anything in it. (laughter) Awareness is receptivity to inspired wisdom. It comes from the Divine Mind.

Student: So, being aware of our invalid ideas is not completely the same as knowing the meaning, is it?

Dr. Hora: The meaning is usually very simple, but most of the time we don't want to know. We are secretive about the meaning of our problems. Now if we are trying to help somebody to know the meaning of the problem we have to be very discreet. And it will preserve us because they will not attack us, whereas secretive people invite attack. People are offended by a secretive individual. He is keeping something for himself and it irritates people. It makes them curious and curiosity is always hostile. So it is not recommended to be secretive. It is highly desirable to be discreet.

Student: You mentioned that it is helpful in understanding the meaning to be willing to be embarrassed.

Dr. Hora: Yes.

Student: On the other hand, if one is assisting someone one is being careful not to embarrass.

Dr. Hora: Okay, but God will embarrass him, and that divine love will embarrass him to the point where he can survive it, bear it, and it will help. It's helpful.

Student: So, being secretive is all those little invalid thoughts in your head?

Dr. Hora: Which "little?" How little?

Student: Well, I was thinking about a friend who professed to want to know about Metapsychiatry, and I haven't talked to her about it for years. Now the secret thought I had about it is that I know something better than you, so . . .

Dr. Hora: That's a good way to lose a friend.

Student: But not talking about it is secretive, yes?

Dr. Hora: Well, if your motivation is to continue enjoying a fantasy that you are smarter than she is because you know something she doesn't know, that's the best way to lose a friend. Pretty soon they will become irritated and hostile and angry.

Student: But in a way it is discreet not to mention Metapsychiatry.

Dr. Hora: Yes, people get very upset when they hear the word Metapsychiatry. They even get upset when they hear the word meaning, because what they want to hear is cause. When you speak of meaning they get upset.

Student: If they hear about meaning through the 11th principle then it is discreet. And if it is one-upmanship it's secretive. So, no response could be discreet or secretive depending on your motivation.

Dr. Hora: Surely.

Student: Dr. Hora, is there any significance to eye contact? Sometimes it is easy to look right in someone's eye and sometimes it isn't so easy. When it isn't easy is that being secretive?

Dr. Hora: No, that's fear. The eyes can communicate hostility, envy, jealousy, malice, rivalry or love, encouragement or sympathy. The eyes speak. Jesus spoke about the eyes. He said, "the eyes are the mirror of the soul," and "if thine eye is single, thy whole body is filled with light, but if thine eye is evil, thy whole body is filled with darkness, and if the light that is in you is darkness, how great is your darkness!" (Matthew 6: 22–23) He said that the light of the body is the eye. So, if you have difficulty looking somebody in the eye, either you have negative thoughts about them or they have negative thoughts about you.

Student: A problem I have is not trusting the awareness. One is so used to thinking that one tends to trust that. So this awareness process, how does one strengthen it and not leave it open to being a gut feeling or a hunch?

Dr. Hora: You have to differentiate between gut feelings, emotions, and thoughts; these never come under the domain of awareness. We say, "I am aware of feeling bad, I am aware of feeling sad or I am aware of feeling afraid," but this is not really awareness. This is just an interpretation of physical experiences. True awareness reveals to us certain thoughts which we entertain unknowingly. When you become aware of certain physical conditions, like fear, sweating, anxiety, anger, joy, pleasure or pain, this is not awareness. This is interpretation of sensory experiences. True awareness comes through a process called inspiration or revelation. Certain ideas reveal themselves to us spontaneously and suddenly we become aware of them. And they come from the Divine Mind. They are qualitatively entirely different, because they are not from the body. So, the student was aware that he had a headache. But this is not a correct word for the headache, since awareness does not tell you that you have a headache. Sensation tells you that you have a headache. In true awareness you become aware of the meaning of the headache, of the hidden thought which is that headache. You see, God cannot inform us of our physical experiences. They are communicated through the sensory system; but the healing realizations come through awareness, and real awareness is the understanding of the meaning of a problem. So the word awareness is used quite often incorrectly. I'm aware of a stomach ache. I'm aware of an itch. It's not really the right word. We interpret our sensations and emotions and we call them awareness, but it is not really real awareness.

Student: But awareness is awareness of thoughts.

Dr. Hora: Yes.

Student: There is something interesting that happens too, because if the thought is discerned, you cannot feel the pain and see the thought at the same time.

Dr. Hora: The pain is the thought.

Student: So once you see the thought there is no need for the pain.

Dr. Hora: You see, the pain is necessary as long as you don't want to see the thought. The moment you are willing to see the thought you don't need the pain, so the pain disappears and the thought appears. Now you see it. Now you don't.

Student: Being aware of the thought does not necessarily mean that you understand the meaning and become healed of it, does it?

Dr. Hora: No. It just prepares you to receive the truth that heals. When we understand the meaning there is immediate relief of sorts, but that is not yet the healing. The healing comes when we correct the thought with the truth.

Student: We've said that things come into our attention but not into our experience. Is there awareness when that happens? Where does this fit into what we are talking about?

Dr. Hora: In order to be true one has to be sufficiently enlightened and catch the meaning before it turns into an experience. Suppose somebody insults us or intimidates us. If you are sufficiently enlightened, you can see these thoughts, sort of coming at you, and by discerning their presence and their intent, there is no need for you to turn it into a physical experience, because, as the Bible says, the understanding will save you. If you have understanding then even though it's coming at you, it doesn't touch you. That's what Einstein was referring to when he said, "Arrows of hate have been shot at me many times, but they never touched me, because they came from a world with which I have nothing in common." That's the protection that enlightenment can give us. We can see these arrows coming and they cannot touch us. It is a very desirable condition to be in.

Student: So an arrow from human to human would hurt, but an arrow to a spiritual being would just keep going.

Dr. Hora: Right. And where it will stop nobody knows. (laughter) That's a wonderful state to be in. Otherwise we are very vulnerable. All over the world people are afraid of each other. They are more afraid of each other than of wild beasts.

Student: People are afraid of people because of secret thoughts?

Dr. Hora: Yes, secret thoughts. What we are afraid of is other people's thoughts. Let's face it. But some of us are more vulnerable to other people's thoughts than others. What makes us vulnerable to other people's thoughts?

Student: The more we are concerned with ourselves.

Dr. Hora: The more we are yearning for good thoughts from other people coming to us, the more we want to be liked, accepted, admired, praised, the more vulnerable we are to criticism, condemnation, rejection, etc. That's why in a family, people are much more touchy and suffer more from each other's thoughts than anywhere else. You see, if Mayor Dinkins thought that you were a lousy character, you wouldn't get scared . . . right? Because it is not important to you to be liked by Mayor Dinkins. But, if it were important to you, you would be very vulnerable. It becomes a precarious situation. Now many people walk around looking for love and affection and praise and admiration, all the time, from anybody, even Mayor Dinkins. Such people are utterly miserable because you can't hardly get them no more — these compliments. (laughter) So it is important not to want, and not to not want. How is that?

Student: It is being issue-oriented?

Dr. Hora: And what is the issue?

Student: Being here for God.

Dr. Hora: Yes, the issue is the issue, always.

Student: Is it possible to be issue-oriented without being aware of your state of consciousness?

Dr. Hora: Yes, if you are fortunate enough to get a good education; I think the legal education is very advantageous, because I think that lawyers are trained to be focused on the issues rather than on personal relationships, and that's a great advantage. When I was in law school, I never learned... (laughter). Psychology renders people extremely vulnerable. It's a great handicap to have had psychological training because you are constantly preoccupied with relationships. And what are relationships but what one person thinks about the other person. And you are always working and working trying to make sure that people like you and have good thoughts towards you. This is a difficult situation. You can't hardly get anybody no more to think good thoughts about you. (laughter)

Student: I was told a story the other day about a man who had a fear of flying. He was told to go see his doctor, and he went to the doctor and the doctor told him not to go because he would have a lousy time. His answer sounded like something a psychologist would say.

Dr. Hora: No, a psychologist would say, just relate yourself the right way to the stewardess and have a few drinks and you will fly. A psychological view of life is, if you don't have good relationships you are miserable, and you have to learn how to influence the relationship in such a way that it would make you feel good. But that is really very sad. Sometimes you get so fed up with this business of relationships that you say, I don't give a damn anymore what people think of me. Will that work?

Student: No, it is the same.

Dr. Hora: You cannot be indifferent. You cannot be callous, because that's a relationship. You cannot avoid contact with people, because that is also a relationship. You cannot stay in it and you cannot run away from it. You can't hardly do anything. There is no solution to life on that level.

Student: So what is the alternative to relationships?

Dr. Hora: Issue-orientedness.

Student: There seems to be enormous attempts in our culture to heal relationships. We see so much on television and books about the inner child, co-dependency, dysfunctional relationships. It all seems to come from this issue about being healed in relationships. You see them talking on television about relationships 30 or 40 years ago and the therapist tells them to write a letter. Interestingly, they say they are trying to heal a wound that they have had their whole life, this persistent pain.

Dr. Hora: They are trying to straighten out a snake! A snake can be straight only when it is dead, and when we are dead, we are free of these concerns about these relationships. In the cemetery there are no more relationships.

Student: Is it the interaction thinking that has to be healed?

Dr. Hora: When we speak of issue-orientedness we have transcended interaction thinking. That's the alternative.

Student: There is neither self...

Dr. Hora: There's neither self nor other; there is only that which really is.

Student: When one realizes that meaning of the thought, whether it be jealousy or whatever and one says, "Wait a minute. This is not right." Is that the awareness of what is?

Dr. Hora: No, that is psychological sophistication. You are always preoccupied with what other people are thinking about you. So you can see one is jealous, one is envious, one is hostile, one is crooked; all kinds of complications prevail while you try to figure out where you stand in relationship to others. Life is very complicated that way. And you have to be secretive because you cannot tell people, "Look here, I know that you are envious of me, I know that you admire me, or I know you hate my guts." There was a time when this was recommended. It was the period of encounter groups when they came together and they thought that if they encouraged each other to tell each other how they felt, this would make people honest. Baloney. Instead of being honest they became rude and cruel with each other and after awhile they saw that this doesn't work. Some people lost their jobs because they learned to be honest. The human condition is the history of stupidity, ignorance and self-damage. The Bible teaches us that love is spiritual and man is spiritual and truth is non-personal, issue oriented, and in the realm of Love-Intelligence there is neither self nor other. There is only that which really is. We spare ourselves a lot of complications and headaches. Every physical symptom is an interaction thought. It is amazing that people have not yet discovered this when this truth is screaming at us. Every painful symptom is an angry interaction thought.

Student: Are the angry interaction thoughts part of being secretive?

Dr. Hora: Well, sometimes we are secretive toward ourselves. If we do not want to know what we are thinking, we are being secretive about our own problems, too. Discretion shall preserve thee, understanding shall save thee and secretiveness shall destroy thee. Self-confirmation is self-destruction and self-destruction is self-confirmation. Don't you think it is good to know this? You get very valuable information here. (laughter)

6

Reaction vs. Response

Student: I am back to work now so I kind of see things a little more sharply, having been away from the situation for a while. I find that I am sensitive to criticism, and I have the idea that people are watching me and they are sort of passing judgment on what I am like and how I do the job, and I feel that it's hostile. You can either ignore it, or you can react or get angry. This is the question I have: What is the healthy response to hostile comments?

Dr. Hora: Does anybody know? How do we deal with hostility? There are two ways that we can deal with it. We can react or we can respond. What is the difference between reaction and response?

Student: I guess reaction is horizontal because it would be interpersonal, and response would be vertical because it is transcending the horizontal perspective and responding to the will of God, which is rising above the whole situation.

Dr. Hora: Yes. If we understand, we are not afraid of hostility. What we do with hostility is analyze it to see its meaning so we don't have to react. There are two possibilities when someone is hostile. In our thoughts we analyze the meaning of the hostility. We don't have to bring it out into the open. We just deal with the meaning and it dissipates itself, because when truth is brought out into the open, there is no reason to react. Remember the Zen Master who was faced with the hostility of a whole community because he was falsely accused? What did he do? He said, "Is that so?" It turned it into a sincere inquiry as to the truth of the situation and there was no problem. But we don't react against hostility. We analyze it.

Student: You are saying what meaning it has for yourself?

Dr. Hora: In general. So if we don't have to react, then there is no boiling over point and everything is just focused and taken apart in an intelligent and quiet way. You don't have to react against hostility. There is plenty of stupid hostility in the world. We don't have to react to it. Will you be able to do it without getting hot under the collar?

Student: You get to think that people are hostile to you and to maintain composure and act friendly, it's —

Dr. Hora: Intelligent, yes. Calmly and intelligently and analytically. It's a much better way. Enlightened people never react to anything. You have no problem if you are able to reveal things that way.

Student: It came to mind that if we didn't have preconceived ideas of who we are and how people should treat us, then it really wouldn't bother us if people were hostile. But it is because we have a certain idea of how things should be, then when they are not that way it becomes very upsetting to us. Is that right? In a way it is really a "should" thought.

Dr. Hora: Of course. A should thought underlies all conflicts, misunderstandings and reactions. Reactions are always personal. Responses are always on the basis of meaning, and are hence meaningful responses. So we don't have to be reactive people. We can be responsive people.

Student: Is there always a should when there is a reaction?

Dr. Hora: Reactions are always personal. Responses are intellectual or wise, intelligent, analytical.

Student: Are they inspired?

Dr. Hora: If you are a sufficiently enlightened individual then you respond with some inspired wisdom from God in every situation.

Student: But not necessarily.

Dr. Hora: No, you can put on some boxing gloves.

Student: Responses are also issue oriented. That is very important in being responsive rather than reacting.

Dr. Hora: Absolutely, right. Issue oriented. Reactions are personal and responses are issue oriented. We are interested in the truth rather than being right or being wrong or feeling this way or feeling that way. It's a wonderful thing to notice. You can learn a lot from watching these talk shows. So you can see how people who don't understand life always react in a personal way and very frequently these people get into physical combat. They start fighting at the drop of a hat and they have to send in muscle men to calm them down. People fight. That is how wars and all kinds of conflicts arise in life. It is very important to understand.

Student: You said before that we have to analyze the situation. It seems to me that some people tend to be critical. Some people are deliberately critical; somehow they seem to have gotten the impression it gives them power to be critical. If you are interested in power, this criticizing gives them a false sense of power, because they sit in a room and they are silently criticizing you, and if you are interested in defending yourself, you are all thumbs by the end of the meeting and they have won. They have won the battle and I have noticed that in that situation the only thing that is helpful is if I don't have a sense of wanting to defend myself, because if I give in to their sense of power, I am overwhelmed. If I do not defend myself, if I am interested in being upright and dignified, then I can just learn to see it and walk away from the meeting not wounded as I normally would be. It is incredible how criticism is very damaging if one believes in it and really gets into it. It's very painful.

Student: But I have to be a person there to receive the criticism. If there is nobody home — (laughter).

Student: Maybe this is just repeating what the other student said, but I have noticed in certain situations if you can identify the value system of another individual, you can see that hostility is a manifestation of that value system, so that it hasn't really anything to do with you at all. It has to do only with the value system being expressed.

Dr. Hora: Yes, that is why often you see that people are talking but they are not listening to each other at all. They are just talking in order to squelch the other one and they want to win. On all these talk shows mostly people go there who want to prove something or to win an argument. That is the issue for them, to win an argument. So there is no dialogue at all. There is just a fight.

Student: So to respond one would have to be mindful of who they really are. They must know the Truth of Being.

Dr. Hora: No, to respond you have to lose all interest in yourself. You are only interested in clearly identifying the issues. Suppose somebody calls you an Irish name. (laughter) Will you explode? Well, you are not interested in the meaning of what is being said. You just want to have the upper hand in an argument.

Student: But if a person hears such a remark, how would they respond in the right way?

Dr. Hora: You start by asking for clarification and you patiently wait until they try to clarify themselves and they hang themselves. (laughter) There is no need to fight.

Student: That could be a clever way to put the other person down.

Dr. Hora: If that is what you are interested in, that is what you will have.

Student: I see.

Dr. Hora: If you are sincerely interested in clarity, then you will not have anything to fight about.

Student: Don't you have to have some sense of who you are, to know the Truth of Being?

Dr. Hora: No. You are nothing. You don't exist. You are not even there. There is an issue there. So we must always focus on the issue and seek to clarify it. Where or when will the world become peaceful? All you see is fighting, fighting, squelching others, preventing them from saying anything, winning. It is very stupid. Cock fights.

Student: If someone is attacking you or criticizing you and you see what is being attempted, it's appropriate to respond to it, right?

Dr. Hora: No. (laughter)

Student: For example, the other day I gave my boss a schedule. She is hostile; it is nothing new. So she called me up and she said, "I would like you to make a change." It was a valid point; she had a different concept, and she said, "Well if you can't understand it like this, you ought to do it like that to make it simple for yourself." And I said to myself, "I have no mind so I am not going to be insulted but I will respond to it," and I said to her, "I can really understand any concept if you would just clarify it." She just stopped and we moved on to the real issue. Was I responding? It just seemed like I had to say something. I was not going to take the insult.

Dr. Hora: You said the right thing. You asked for clarification. Who can argue against that?

Student: Because afterwards I just did what she asked for and I didn't feel wounded. It's not my mind anyway. (laughter) So we respond by seeking clarity in the situation. That's the motivation.

Dr. Hora: That's all. Nobody can take issue with that.

Student: We don't have to worry about knowing our identity because all those thoughts seem to be overwhelming. Your identity doesn't exist. You ain't never was nothing. So what identity are you talking about?

Student: I got a call from one of the bosses, and after we finished the conversation, I couldn't understand what the purpose of that call was. The secretary called saying, "Mr. So-and-So wants to talk to you," and then he came on the line and I said "Yes." He said, "Well, what's up?" Then he started in with "What are you doing? That's not the way." No matter what I said it was wrong. He went on for five minutes and that was the end of it. It was obviously hostile. There was no rhyme or reason for this.

Dr. Hora: He was hung up in embarrassment and frustration. He tried to pick a fight with you and didn't know how to do it.

Student: It stayed with me for the next 24 hours that someone would go to the trouble to get me. He is out to get me.

Dr. Hora: That's a mistake. He probably had a fight with his wife in the morning and wanted to take it out on you.

Student: It is hard to respond when it is so blatant an attack.

Student: He was away from work for a long time. It seems in a work environment everyone is always trying to position themselves, and if a boss is calling he wants to reestablish his bossiness. I see people doing that after a vacation. They come back like gangbusters. They come back and want to make sure you know that they are back, so you just let them be. It just seems like that's the way of the world. It's nothing personal really. They have to establish their position. Isn't it important for us to see these issues, because you analyze the situation and it isn't personal?

Dr. Hora: The issue was a desire to say, "I am your boss. I am superior to you." You don't argue about that.

Student: But even that thought could be comforting; so we don't walk away feeling wounded or attacked. They don't mean it personally half the time...right? I guess when we see these situations, if we can see it from their perspective, is that helpful?

Dr. Hora: The Bible says, "Agree with thine adversary quickly, whiles thou art in the way with him" (Matthew 5:25). Before an argument develops, before it turns into a fight, you agree with him. That's all, and then there is no fight and things calm down. Agree with thine adversary quickly. Most primitive people who have never studied Metapsychiatry assume that every conversation has to culminate in a fight because it is the adversarial viewpoint on life.

Student: The difficult part is when it stays in your mind where it keeps going on over and over for 24 hours...and he said and I said.

Dr. Hora: You have not understood that you are an issue oriented, responsive individual and there is no need to be seduced into controversy.

Student: These lessons are very difficult.

Dr. Hora: If you want anything except the truth. We are not interested in anything else but the truth. When we speak of clarity, we mean that we are interested in clarifying the issues so that the truth may emerge.

Student: I suppose we could ask ourselves, "What is there to like?" The real answer to that would be nothing.

Dr. Hora: Well, you are a nice girl. We like you.

Student: You are in the minority. (laughter)

Student: There is a tendency to take the criticism seriously and prove the criticizers wrong.

Dr. Hora: Cock fights. This is very unpleasant.

Student: In Art History class the professor showed slides and one of the students questioned, "What made this slide great?" She didn't think this was a great work of art, and immediately the professor took it as a personal criticism and they got into a fight, a verbal confrontation over whether this was a great work of art or not. Neither of them could back down and end it. It went on for about 15 minutes and it was just embarrassing for the rest of the class. There was no clarification; it was just a matter of who was right.

Student: When I look at a situation at a work site, I have a tendency to be very negative. I am the one being critical, not outwardly, but I'm very saddened by what is going on. It seems to be worsening. If I could say, "So what, it's none of my business and only the way that it appears" and leave it, it would be okay. But I am not able to let go that way. I know about it. Do I need to look for good in the situation or do I just really need to let it go? It's not my business.

Dr. Hora: Well, you ask yourself, "What is it in me that wants to criticize and agree and disagree; what is the meaning of this inclination?" And then you will know: it is the urge for self-confirmatory ideation. You see it everywhere there is conflict. They would like to confirm themselves by being right, by being admired or winning arguments. There is no need to do that. You cannot get the Nobel Prize this way; it is too hard to fight for it.

Student: I think what I hear you saying is that we also have to be certain not to be critical and to let people be whatever they are at whatever level of understanding they have, and not to be judgmental. In a work place sometimes there are situations where you need to depend on someone else's work to complete your work. There seems to be that aspect of it. If they don't deliver something, I tend to be critical, because it seems to me that people can't stay focused sometimes. They get so preoccupied with all the interactions in the workplace, and whenever I depend on someone for something I get critical. I find it difficult. It seems like I need something from them to do my work.

Dr. Hora: Do you really need it or do you just attempt to assert your personal importance?

Student: Well, the way it is structured is for me to do the consolidation. I need everybody's piece before I can consolidate it and then do the analysis. So, yes I need that to provide me with —

Dr. Hora: You have to go with a piece. You know what a piece is? It's a gun. (laughter) That would be most appropriate in an adversarial situation.

Student: I am always struggling with the idea that God is in control, that God is the harmonizing principle, and then that's fine and I calm down. But then I realize it's getting closer and closer to deadline and I am still waiting. So right away I become critical again. Are these experiences just opportunities to learn the lesson that we have to lean on God and then it just doesn't matter? Then if the work or whatever is not completed because of certain things, it doesn't really matter. It's not a reflection on me.

Dr. Hora: Sure. What is the meaning of our life? To come to know the truth — they are all opportunities to learn.

Student: So if we are critical we are just not learning our lesson in that situation. It's a copout: it's an easy way out. It's easy to criticize.

Dr. Hora: It is unpleasant, isn't it, after we have made the mistake of criticizing or being personally involved with somebody? Always be careful not to get adversarial.

Student: It seems like some people at work look for that; they thrive on it. I marvel at how people set themselves up for that.

Dr. Hora: It's a common thing, in our culture particularly, to view every situation as an adversarial situation when the issue is to win. The real issue gets lost and everybody just gets ready to win an argument, a fight to show that we are more knowledgeable than others.

Student: Everything that we have talked about today always ends up with our should thinking, like the people should have those reports ready for me so I can get my work done. The second principle is always appearing and reminding me what should be and what shouldn't be.

Dr. Hora: How people should be or they shouldn't be. Everything is personal.

Student: So seeing the good of God —

Dr. Hora: There is another thought which is prevalent: my progress, my promotion, my career depends on winning, proving that we are better, that we are superior. So everybody is an enemy and nobody gives a damn about the truth. The truth usually gets lost because fighting takes over, and if we win we succeed in making additional enemies. If we lose, they have enemies in us. We hate them because we are losers. This is life in an adversarial culture.

The other day I was watching on TV an Indian doctor who came from India to the U.S. and studied in the University of Virginia. He was extremely well educated and he could talk beautifully. For several hours he was talking on TV without once mentioning anything about himself. There was no self in his lecture. It was very beautiful. Dr. Deepak Chopra. No notes, nothing. Never any self referential remarks. He was very clear. It was a pleasure to watch him and to hear him. He was truly a well educated doctor, which is very rare.

Student: Just a few weeks ago he had a meeting and packed the hall. He has a sense of humor and he would say things like, "you think that that's a chair right there, but that is not the reality." He could put things over. He said he was able to say that, after his earlier writings which were very medically oriented, he had moved in another direction.

Dr. Hora: Yes, he is completely spiritual and that is good and all his education is just a way of presenting truth which is beyond the truth of conventional medical teaching. He is an unusual man, beyond the truth of conventional medicine. Deepak Chopra — it's a very strange name.

Student: Did you hear what he said? He was in a room where people had cancer and the doctors would come and sit down and give them a report about what their blood count was or how they were improving or not. When they said the name and they said something negative about the report, the person would get sick and look down, and get fearful and discouraged. When they said, "Your report is good," the person was well and strong and sitting up, and he showed how important our thoughts are.

Dr. Hora: A good doctor is a good doctor because he went beyond being a doctor. It was clearly demonstrated in his case. All his values were spiritual even though he was well educated in materialistic medicine. He tried to demonstrate the validity of spiritual values and ideas. He used the traditional ways of thinking to bring it into contrast with the spiritual. It is a very, very intelligent way to teach.

Student: Also he wasn't on the podium talking to the people; he was amongst the people. He was very funny.

Student: The acceptance of this is wonderful.

Dr. Hora: That's a good point.

Student: Last Tuesday night, Andrew Weil — who is also a medical doctor and authored the book *Spontaneous Healing*...spoke without notes. Not so profoundly as Deepak, but again: what you believe is what happens. He has studied healing all over the world. He said first he had to get his credentials. He graduated from Harvard Medical School and was associated with good organizations but now he is not afraid. Now they are sending doctors to him, after they are trained, for him to undo some of their training.

Student: As adversarial as this world is, there are still people who are seeking enlightenment and truth in spite of everything.

Dr. Hora: This Deepak Chopra wasn't talking about healing. He was talking about what is real and how the right understanding of reality heals. But when you talk about healing, you are putting yourself in the same situation as a traditional doctor. A doctor gets paid for his work. It consists of trying to find out what the sickness is and how to heal it. But there is no healing of sicknesses because there is no sickness. There is just the truth or nothing, because God is never sick. Trying to cure a sick person means that you acknowledge that there is sickness and there is health, and you try to fight against sickness and achieve health. God knows nothing about this nonsense. There is no sickness in God's reality and there is no health. What is there?

Student: Perfection.

Dr. Hora: Who said that? We have to be careful about what we say because it might turn out that we are saying the truth as a lie. What happens when we say the truth and we are lying?

Student: What do you mean, "When we are saying the truth and we are lying?"

Dr. Hora: That is what I asked. (laughter) You say the truth and you don't really know it, and you are just pretending and you are a liar. You are using the truth to lie. You can tell a charlatan right away. A charlatan is a fake; he is faking it. He read it in a book or he heard it in a lecture but he never really understood. But with this Chopra guy, he was talking about things that are very difficult for even a well-trained medical doctor to really know, and you didn't have that sense that he is lying with the truth. He was just very authentic, a genuine scientist who really knows the truth. The fake knowers cause a lot of trouble because they just talk about the truth and pretend to understand what they are talking about, and the result is that everybody gets confused and irritated. So one has to be very careful with the truth. We have no right to talk about the truth unless we really understand it.

Student: And demonstrate it as well. It is one thing to understand it, and if we don't demonstrate it in our lives we are still charlatans.

Dr. Hora: Yes, sure. That is right. So we have to be careful.

Student: You spoke in the context of spiritual ideas. How can we communicate in the world without calling attention to ourselves, without using "I" or "me?" It seems difficult.

Dr. Hora: It's very important. It's called self-transcendence, to rise above the self-confirmatory element in our thinking.

Student: We could be grateful for being able to do a task and say, "Here, I did this." But in saying "I did this," that is self-confirmatory.

Dr. Hora: Yes, that is an elementary mistake, Mr. Watson. (laughter)

Student: Could you give me an example? The work is done, period. Here it is; it's all done.

Student: There is a teacher in our department who has been looking for another job. The phone rang and some man from another school was calling this individual. Later in the day I was walking through the hall and I saw him in a classroom. I asked him, "Did you get the message?" He said, "Oh, thanks, it's important." I delivered the message that is going to help this guy to get a job in another school. I was just a messenger. I delivered this message verbally to this guy. I was just one of the lines of communication, so to speak.

Dr. Hora: Did you pin a medal on yourself? (laughter)

Student: I tried hard. (laughter) But you could be just a channel for communication.

Dr. Hora: You ain't never was nothing.

Student: You said a few minutes ago that we have no right to speak about the truth if you don't really understand it, for then we would be charlatans. What about in prayer or meditation? It seems like we have to start with some principle or some idea that we may not understand. What's the difference?

Dr. Hora: You have the principles and you contemplate the principles without speaking them out to anybody else. The danger is that when we get impressed that we know something valuable, we are charlatans. We cannot show off with what we know.

Student: How do we know when we are trying to do that to ourselves during prayer?

Dr. Hora: You will know because you will feel like a prostitute in church. (laughter) Anybody who does it is really defiling himself.

Student: A lot of the talk is about work and school — anywhere. This summer there was a retirement incentive offered, and when I thought of not working at the job, it brought up many issues and concerns. Now as I am working, I think about the fact that I didn't take the incentive. I am concerned about how I view work. For economic reasons one has to work, but that is not very valid. There needs to be a little bit more informed way of looking at work.

Dr. Hora: What could that be?

Student: I need your help.

Dr. Hora: You are asking me? (laughter) I can recommend a little book for you. It explains the meaning and purpose of work. What is that book? *Right Usefulness.*

There are two issues in teaching: one is imparting the truth about some subject matter, and the other is demonstrating non-personal, non-conditional benevolence. The subject matter is a vehicle of knowledge that has to be expressed sincerely and in unadulterated form. The other issue is to be a model of spiritual integrity in teaching. So we mentioned this Chopra guy. He was a model of a man who could quietly and sincerely clarify very difficult, scientific issues so as to make them clear to the audience without glorifying himself in the process. So you could learn about the truth and you could observe the truth in action. "He that hath seen me hath seen the Father" (John 14:9) for "I and my Father are one" (John 10:30). That's right usefulness. Not only do you have to know the three Rs but you also have to know your purpose for the situation. So you disappear and the real issues become clear. You're teaching geography and the students see God. That is the right way.

Student: Getting back to the example that was given earlier about the art teacher who was showing the slides. If the teacher had been interested in clarifying the ideas of art, then wouldn't that have been manifested?

Dr. Hora: What motivates somebody to produce works of art? Money? No? (laughter)

7

The Greatest Protection

Student: A question has come up at work concerning the difference between gossip and gathering necessary information. It so happens that recently I've been in the process of putting together a team of people to work on something, and it's done in an atmosphere that is swirling with gossip. After hearing the definitions of gossip, I am concerned about it. Yet I am not always sure how to distinguish motives. When my motive is to enable me to assemble a team, and to determine when someone could be part of that because of their work background, I'm not sure whether I am simply participating in gossip. Is there a valid time to discuss other people in a professional setting?

Dr. Hora: Do we all know what gossip is? What is gossip?

Student: When one or more persons are talking about another person behind their back for their own entertainment.

Dr. Hora: Yes. In other words, it's a person talking about another person or persons to a third person. This is the essential element in gossip. And gossip is a problem, even though it is highly entertaining, and people love to engage in it. But this is a personal viewpoint on life. We see ourselves as persons and we are interested in others as persons. We like to talk about personal lives and personal problems. Everything personal becomes problematic. Now the question is, "How can we live in society, in a community, in a group, without gossiping?" Even in our thoughts we are fantasizing about others. We look at each other and we think, "How do they look? What are they wearing? What are they saying?" We constantly speculate about others. This is so widespread that it is almost considered inevitable and unavoidable. So what's the answer? Is it possible to exist in this world without gossiping? Especially at work, or in families, everybody minds everybody else's business . . . right? Well what's the solution?

Student: Giving up a sense of personhood. Gossip is very personal. So until we are able to see ourselves and others as spiritual beings, we will continue to gossip, even if it's only within our thoughts.

Student: I just thought that these things, like how people dress and what they do . . . you can't help but notice them. But if we don't take an interest in them, we let go of the gossip in that way. We don't dwell on it.

Student: Is this being issue oriented?

Dr. Hora: What is the issue?

Student: Non-personal, such as work issues.

Dr. Hora: No issues but shoes. (laughter) Yes, being issue oriented is part of this, but the true remedy for gossip is perfect love. Have we ever heard of perfect love? In what way does perfect love eliminate gossip altogether? Once we have learned to love perfectly and appreciate loving perfectly, there is a complete abolishing of gossip.

Student: Well, gossip is always condemnatory in one way or another, such as finding fault or ridiculing.

Dr. Hora: It can be admiring too...

Student: Which is secretly envying.

Dr. Hora: You could also say I appreciate this person.

Student: Sometimes it is a way of masking our motive and gaining dominion over another, whereas the idea of love as good will toward individuals would eliminate that. If love is uppermost, then the concern is toward perceiving good will and being aware of it, and the interest in gossip disappears.

Dr. Hora: Well, what if someone says, "I like the way he or she parts her hair." It is important to learn to understand the value of perfect love. First of all, perfect love casts out fear; perfect love abolishes judgmentalism; perfect love frees us from criticism, gossip, prejudice, intolerance. All kinds of problems disappear from our lives, once we have discovered and look at life through the lens of perfect love. How is that?

Student: It is a non-conditional aspect...

Dr. Hora: Non-personal, non-conditional and benevolent. If you are imbued with this understanding, you could not possibly be interested in gossip or the four horsemen or anything else. You become a very dull guy. (laughter)

Student: A wallflower. (laughter)

Student: Is beholding the same as loving perfectly?

Dr. Hora: If we are beholding an individual?

Student: Instead of looking at them critically, or to see what he is wearing, or all those things that are considered gossip.

Dr. Hora: Well it is even more than that, because it is a generalized way of looking at life. We don't focus on individuality. We focus on values. Perfect love focuses on values and focuses on them benevolently. Perfect love makes it possible to be compassionate, to be peaceful, to be unafraid, to be constructive, to participate in life as a beneficial presence. Everything becomes transformed, spiritualized, healed and liberated from the complicated entanglements that the mind is capable of. It is a simple statement: non-personal, nonconditional benevolence. Nothing more is needed except to put it into practice.

Student: Well what is the practice? Is it just thinking those thoughts in the midst of people gossiping around us?

Dr. Hora: Yes. If other people gossip, it is none of our business. Our business is to love perfectly. This is what God wants and we are here for God. When we love perfectly, *we* don't do it. It is God in us that is expressing itself as perfect love.

Student: There is still some confusion. I am not thinking of the things that are so obviously gossip, but the things that come disguised as professional talk in the name of being issue oriented, in the name of being task oriented. I am uncomfortable frequently, and find that I don't see the distinction between what is and what is not gossip.

Dr. Hora: You just have to learn perfect love. There is no other remedy to this.

Student: Let's say we are sitting with our thoughts, and someone comes to mind. If just the thought about another individual comes to mind...

Dr. Hora: Yes, you have to be very careful and radically sincere, and become aware of what you are thinking and constantly reject personal or critical or judgmental or fearful thoughts. Sometimes we think thoughts we are afraid of, or like or dislike. They are always personal thoughts. When we indulge in personal thoughts, even if there is nobody around, we are gossiping.

Student: So, if at that moment we can turn our attention to perfect love, then...

Dr. Hora: Right, every time you sincerely remind yourself of what perfect love is, everything changes. All the other thoughts disappear from consciousness and you find yourself at peace, satisfied. As the Bible says, "I shall behold thy face in righteousness, and I shall be satisfied when I awake with thy likeness" (Psalms 17:15). What does that mean? But who wants to be satisfied? We want to be excited, no? We want to have power.

Student: Does it mean to behold God as the source of perfect love and thus be satisfied with people?

Dr. Hora: Exactly. When we realize it, we will be at peace and satisfied. Otherwise we are always dissatisfied, jumpy, irritable and critical.

Student: Well, at work we are required to fill out personnel files, personnel development forms and evaluations. It is a never ending battle. It is hard sometimes to see how to manifest perfect love when we are asked to find specific weaknesses, because the forms invite you to be critical. And I find it difficult, because even if you stick to the issue, you are still making a negative statement about someone. For example, they need improvement in this area or that. How can perfect love be helpful in these situations where this work is required? You have to do it. The forms sort of force you to find some weakness. No one is perfect under their standards.

Dr. Hora: Yes, but love is perfect.

Student: I don't get it.

Dr. Hora: Well, how do we fill out these forms? Do they ask you to be bitchy and malicious? (laughter) It is all right to criticize performance and point out ways to make desirable improvement, but it is not personal. Of course, you call them "personal evaluations." This is certainly a difficulty for someone who aspires to perfect love. Our culture is imbued with malicious ways of reporting on one another.

Student: Right now the whole personnel function is evaluating everything to streamline operations. Every job is being evaluated and all the supervisors have to go through this. It is not easy, as it is one form after another. It is all on a personal level. The questions are all geared to finding fault so that the company can look to eliminate employees.

Dr. Hora: Right. Recently I saw a little sketch on television where a man was sitting on a park bench. Another man approached and started a conversation with this man who was sitting on the bench. The man who was standing said, "I have a very difficult job." The other man asked, "What do you do?" He said, "I am a Jew catcher." "What is a Jew catcher?" "I catch Jews to report to the authorities that they are still around." This was in Nazi Germany. He said, "This is my occupation, and if I don't catch 10 Jews a week, then they will eliminate me. If I want to survive, I have to run around and work every day until I make my quota of Jews and report them to the authorities for their elimination. So I am a Jew catcher."

So here is a man who is in a job where he is required to find and to report people who then are murdered in the concentration camps. This is a very interesting scene which has far reaching consequences for people, because, while the Nazi solution of employment is very radical and drastic and can give you the shivers that such things are possible, people are put into situations where they are required to be devastatingly evil. So in this film, it was understandable that the Nazis would use a Jew to catch other Jews for extermination. And that was his job. From morning to night he performed his job so that he could survive. He would say "I have to confess to you; I am a Jew myself." So they hired a Jew to catch other Jews for extermination. Now if you work for Citibank, they hire you to report on incompetent employees...right? You yourself are an employee and live in fear of being eliminated, but they expect you to fill out forms which will then help them to eliminate other employees. It is not so far removed from the Jew catcher. Can you see that? It is a horrible thing that such cultural idiocies are accepted as common practice.

Now on another level, there are parents who bring up their children to be a certain way. For instance, let's say you are a white supremacist. Then you will expect your children to bring home information that will hurt blacks in the community or report them to the police. The whole culture manifests such human misery. The human mind is so imbued with evil and malice that the whole culture is just a variation on the situation where man is used to hurt other men. There is a lot of that in the world. So this Jew catcher went along to save his own life; he was willing to work for the Nazis and to report on other Jews who then were exterminated, and this way he could survive for another week.

What would you have done in such a situation, where your own survival depended on the murder of others? In small ways we are brought up and hired and employed to do similar things. Now this man said that he is also a Jew, and that he wants to live, and he has to do this. But there are people who volunteer for these kinds of functions. Nobody asks them to do it, but they somehow are imbued with the thought that one man's loss is another man's gain. Of course, here we see that there is absolutely no trace that there is such a thing as perfect love, (singing) that "what the world needs now..." (laughter) is love. Perfect love... yes? Because under the disguise of love, many malicious acts are perpetrated. If you would ask a thousand people in the street, "Do you know what perfect love is? Have you ever heard of it?" they would say, "Yeah, I read about it in the Bible. It says 'Perfect love casteth out fear' [1 John 4:18]. I know. I know my Bible." But they have no idea what it is and what it could do to the world if people understood and appreciated perfect love. Unfortunately, the Bible doesn't explain what perfect love is. We have to receive it through inspiration to understand it, and that, of course, throws an entirely different light on life.

Now, if this man, this Jew catcher, would have understood perfect love, two things could have happened — he would have volunteered to enter the extermination camp himself or God would have found a way of saving him. But he didn't know. What you don't know *can* hurt you and can hurt many others. So if we are in a job where we are required to malign and hurt our co-workers, we have two things we can do. We can say, "No, I refuse to hurt anybody," or "I resign and I'll go on welfare." But you do absolutely not accept this kind of assignment because you are committed to perfect love, and God will not let you down. I can give it to you in writing. If nothing else happens, you can hang it on the wall. I am sure you all know that God would not let us down if we take a stand on perfect love.

Student: Did this man have to know what his real life was, because he thought his life depended on his catching ten Jewish men to be exterminated?

Dr. Hora: That's all he knew. He was solely concerned with survival. So we try to survive week after week.

Student: And sometimes we think our job is our life.

Dr. Hora: That's a very good point. Sometimes we think we have to be malicious, we have to gossip, we have to hurt people, so that we can save our job. But the job is not life. It is a means for providing for the daily necessities.

Student: Today I got a quarterly report from one of these companies. In it, they talk about how they have increased productivity, eliminated so many employees, and the working profits went up. In the name of efficiency, isn't there a place for making a company more productive and efficient, eliminating waste and things like that?

Dr. Hora: Well, that is a different issue. It is not malice. It does not say that we have required our employees to make malicious reports on their colleagues so that we could eliminate them. They probably asked an expert in productivity to make a study and find ways to streamline how they were working. And of course, decent companies also provide outplacement help for people who have become surplus in a certain area, finding them new jobs, providing severance pay and ways to take care of them that are quite humane. But this student is reporting something that doesn't look very nice. If it is required of you by these questionnaires to be tricky and to expect you to be malicious toward your colleagues, you don't have to accept it.

Student: Can't you fudge it? Say something without saying anything.

Dr. Hora: You can fudge it to a certain extent, especially if you like chocolate fudge.

Student: It reminds me of school where tattling is widespread. There is one class in particular where the kids love to tattle on each other and tell the teacher.

Dr. Hora: Yes, but tattling has been in general disapproval in the schools, hasn't it?

Student: Well, it may not be encouraged, but it is very widespread.

Dr. Hora: Yes.

Student: To get back to the idea of perfect love as being necessary, how do you rise above what you see, when you see people acting in a malicious way all the time, and that is in direct conflict with the mandate to love perfectly? The words are so easy. We say we have to understand that these people are ignorant, and we have to look at these people with compassion. We have to love them perfectly. I mean, this Jew catcher had to look at these people who were telling him what to do and he had to look at them with perfect love.

Dr. Hora: Nobody has mentioned that we have to look at people with perfect love.

Student: To love perfectly is not personal.

Dr. Hora: Right, we don't love people. Perfect love does not focus on people, persons and individuals. Perfect love focuses on love, on being beneficial, loving presences in the world. It is non-personal, non-conditional benevolence.

Student: Okay then, what then? How do you respond when you see malicious acts being performed by persons.

Dr. Hora: If you are a policeman, you arrest them. If you are not a policeman, you just remain loving and God will arrest them. (laughter)

Student: I guess that really is the question. Is it possible to remain loving in that environment?

Dr. Hora: The fantastic thing about perfect love is that it precludes interaction thinking, and you all know that all our difficulties in life come from interaction thinking.

Student: I would like you to clarify. We don't *do* perfect love; we just understand there *is* perfect love?

Dr. Hora: Yes, our consciousness has to be imbued with the idea of perfect love, and the whole world is changed.

Student: Dr. Hora, it seems that to get beyond interaction thinking, we would have to keep reminding ourselves over and over all the time, because it seems that there is a deep-seated reactivity in our being that is almost impossible to overcome. Something happens and, before we know it, we already have a personal response. But we can catch ourselves and work with it. So when we think about perfect love, the idea of seeing everything as phenomena and the idea of perfect love seem very difficult.

Dr. Hora: Well, we'll give you a time period. When the disciples asked Jesus, "How many times do we have to forgive our enemies, seven times?" Jesus said, "Seventy times seven." We just have to work with the idea until we see more and more the practical value of being imbued with perfect love. One of the Metapsychiatric principles says, "If you know what, you know how." So we work on knowing what it is. What is perfect love? When we are imbued with this, we will know how. The quality of our presence will be a living expression of perfect love. And this is an accomplishment fervently to be desired.

Now, for instance, if the student who is required to evaluate her fellow employees goes to work making sure that she is filled with a desire to be a perfectly loving consciousness, many things can happen. Good things can happen. The demands on her ways of reporting may be rescinded, or may be changed, or God can inspire her with such wisdom and the right words to put down so that it will be a good report and it will hurt no one. There is a Latin saying, "Nil nocere." What does that mean? Above all, never to hurt. This is a medical command that I remember from medical school. Doctors are admonished that they are in practice as physicians to keep thinking, above all, not to hurt the patient. Be careful never to hurt the patient. You see, I have forgotten this, and apparently the other doctors have also forgotten. (laughter)

Student: They've forgotten, but you've been healed. (laughter)

Student: What's likely to happen in a situation like this if one took a moral or ethical stand?

Dr. Hora: This is neither moral nor ethical. This is spiritual. Moral is religious; ethical is human; perfect love is spiritual. So many good things invariably happen when we understand and are committed to perfect love.

Student: If we see lots of malice, what does that indicate? Does that mean that we ourselves are malicious or that we just don't understand enough about love?

Dr. Hora: If we see ourselves surrounded by malice, then we will either like it or dislike it. If we like it, we're sunk. If we dislike it, we are also sunk. So what else is there?

Student: Not to be interested, but to allow ourselves to be interested in perfect love.

Dr. Hora: Right. We are unimpressed by malice, by jealousy, by rivalry, by gossip, by envy. All of these are human ways of thinking and acting.

Student: And most of the human ways have an intent to hurt.

Dr. Hora: Yes, of course, to be human is hurtful. Well, we are all here to learn that we are not really meant to be human. We are not really meant to be animalistic, right? We are meant to be spiritual, and that spiritual consciousness loves perfectly. And perfect love awakens within us the spirituality of our consciousness and good things can happen. When we are merely human or animal we are just a miserable hit or miss proposition. Then we are believers in luck, lady luck. We are gamblers, drug addicts, Jew catchers. This scene impressed me very much — the evil that man is sometimes driven to get himself involved with. And, of course, in Germany this was not unusual.

Student: If our consciousness is imbued with perfect love, there is no object toward which we're being perfectly loving. But I have trouble understanding this. I always think in terms of loving something.

Dr. Hora: No, we love being loving because God is love. So when we have learned perfect love, we are actualizing the truth that we are transparencies through whom God is manifesting in the world. When you have achieved this clear understanding, you can expect all kinds of things to happen to you and around you, every day, or even at night. This is the total realization of at-one-ment with the Divine Mind. It erases the human traits and the animal traits. Previously, we mentioned here that the vast majority of people exist on the animal level or the human level, and not on a spiritual level.

Student: So if someone says something malicious to us, we would not be interested in what they said. I get hung up on seeing them as a transparency for God, for instance, which seems to have an object, whereas perfect love would be more concerned with just being loving, not just seeing that person as a transparency. I guess I am confused here.

Dr. Hora: It is impossible to see an evil man as a transparency. We could theorize about it ... yes? So we are not trying to delude ourselves that an evil is not evil. We see the evil. It is not like the three monkeys who see no evil, hear no evil, speak no evil. That's not what we are about. We are about immunity. We have immunity from all these evils through the grace of God. And this immunity is ours to the extent that we are in the consciousness of perfect love. So we see these things, but we are unimpressed, unafraid, disinterested and compassionate. We can have compassion, which is a tremendous thing, which liberates us from interacting with these evil things. At the same time, it is a blessing to the one who is not sufficiently advanced and doesn't even have the idea that it is possible to love perfectly. Most people do not know this. The greatest protection in life is perfect love, compassion. It eliminates interaction thinking. It eliminates relationships. You don't get entangled with anybody and nobody gives a damn about you.

Student: Other than that, it's great. (laughter)

Dr. Hora: No, actually, any individuals who have attained the mode of being of perfect love find that people very much appreciate their presence and that wherever they go people are drawn to them.

Student: Just as you said, "true love has no object." Therefore, God does not love us.

Dr. Hora: It is a religious compromise when we say God loves you. Most people are not able to understand how love exists without an object. Psychoanalysis has elevated the concept of love-object to a level of scientific prestige. But there is really no such thing. If you say to someone, "I love you," you are not only lying, but you are also reducing that individual to the level of an object. This is called reification. It is not deification, but it is a reification, which means making him or her into a thing.

8

Reverence for Life

Student: Dr. Hora, last week we were talking about compassion vs. condescension. This week I have been reading some Buddhist stories that showed some severe examples of people being compassionate after being blinded or mutilated. I tried to reflect back on situations where I am not being compassionate, even though I am not having severe problems. I tried to understand why there is great difficulty in trying to be compassionate when you see these examples of people under worse situations doing so, and I don't have an answer for the question. Are they just stories that seem to be true that we read in this literature? If somebody blinded me, I doubt I could be compassionate, even if someone does something or we perceive something to be done of a lesser nature.

Dr. Hora: This literature — I don't know what you were reading, but usually Buddhist literature has a purpose of educating people towards having a more valid outlook on life, and, as a result of that, their responses to all kinds of experiences heal them. The point is to find the valid, intelligent, harmonious way of coping with life. Compassion is very helpful, primarily to the compassionate one. You are not doing a favor for somebody if you are compassionate. You are really helping yourself to find this equanimity, this peace which enlightened thought can bring to you. It is good to be good, right? Unbelievable as it sounds. People will say it is crazy to be good in a world which is so evil. But we say it is good to be good. It is not good to be judgmental and critical and vindictive and hateful and aggressive. Those things are not good for anybody. So, if you read this Buddhist literature, you can see that the writers, and the enlightened man they describe, are always interested in helping people — to help people by illuminating, for them, the Truth of Being.

Student: The solutions or the realizations always happen to the blind or crippled. The situation doesn't represent your spiritual values. You are beyond that, so it is not a problem for those individuals.

Dr. Hora: The Buddhists don't talk about love. It does not appear as much as in Christianity, but they do talk about compassion a lot and that is very helpful. Suppose you have to spend four days with your mother-in-law and she is not a very enlightened woman and she curses or spits or criticizes, and is generally negative about you. If you have compassion you won't suffer. If you don't have compassion you will suffer a lot just from the companionship. People are hurting a lot.

Student: In the illustration you gave, what's the compassionate way if somebody is cursing or being vile? What is the right thought?

Dr. Hora: It indicates that the individuals are not aware of what is good, what is loving, what is beneficial. They are judging by appearances.

Student: In the same context I had a question about the non-personal aspect of Perfect Love. It seems like a lot of times (maybe it is a mistake) when Perfect Love comes to mind, we are thinking about an individual wherein there isn't so much perfect love. I mean it's a difficult situation. Instead of being viewed with this loving orientation, a lot of times what happens is when we are with somebody it is hard to remind ourselves of non-personal, non-conditional benevolence. But then it seems like, because we are thinking about that person, that individual, then it's personal.

Dr. Hora: That's a very good point. I was just going to say that in Buddhism they do not think in terms of self and other. When they speak about compassion, they don't think "I am going to be compassionate towards him." It is not an interactional idea. But in western culture, psychology is completely contaminated and everyone is imbued with the idea of relationships. You don't have to be involved in an interpersonal relationship with anyone, and you can be loving. It is the love of being loving, not the love for somebody. We don't love anybody; we just love being loving and that is freedom, because if you misunderstand love in terms of relationships, then you are entangled. "Stand fast therefore in the liberty wherewith Christ hath made us free, and be not entangled again with the yoke of bondage" (Galatians 5:1). Here we speak about bonding. Have you ever heard this term bonding? What does it say?

Student: It says self and other.

Dr. Hora: Yes, you get bonded with somebody, which means you go crazy about being with that person or loving him or her.

You get sort of entangled with some individual. Everybody — including psychologists — is always talking about bonding as if it were something very good. We feel good occasionally or for a little bit. But after a while you see that you are a prisoner of this emotional entanglement. The idea is that if you are not bonded with anybody, then you will be a loner and that is another dreadful thing in our culture. It is a frightening idea because loners are what psychologists call schizoid. People who are afraid of being near other people are considered loners, and since we are so involved in dualistic thinking, we cannot find the answer to this problem. Either you are entangled with somebody or you are a loner, right? In either case, you suffer. It is not good to be entangled and it's not good to be a loner. So what is good?

Student: We were thinking of compassion and love.

Dr. Hora: Right, non-personal, non-conditional benevolence and forgiveness and letting be. It is hard for ordinary people to transcend the dualism of relationships or non-relationships.

Student: It seems to be a big phenomenon in papers these days that the loners are trying to meet people. There are pages and pages of people writing in, wishing to meet, and to me it is very pathetic.

Dr. Hora: That is a psychological attempt at solving this problem and if you don't know any alternative, that's what you're stuck with. There is no third alternative. This is the western culture. But Buddhism has led us to the revelation of the teachings of Jesus, which says: "Love being loving." Don't get entangled with people and don't shy away from people. Remain loving, because the third alternative is Divine Love,

Perfect Love, non-conditional benevolence. There is a third alternative but nobody knows about it, and that is what we are talking about.

Student: The situation that comes to mind involves Asian children that I see in school. They don't crave interaction the way the American children do. They can be friendly or they can be alone, but mostly the American children crave interaction so intensely that there is constant conflict.

Dr. Hora: You have many Asian children now in school?

Student: The more the better.

Dr. Hora: You like them!

Student: Well, every teacher does. They are wonderful students.

Dr. Hora: It is very sad with the American kids. They don't know these things.

Student: Is there a value that is taught in Asian families?

Dr. Hora: I don't know, but where else would they get it? It's tradition, I think. It is the Buddhist and Hindu traditions. Taoism, Hinduism, and Buddhism all teach the non-dual nature of reality.

Student: Do we as adults seek to understand that? Do we see everything in dualistic terms? Is that a major issue?

Dr. Hora: It's a major handicap in seeing and responding to life. Everything is black and white. You hear it all the time. It's either black or white. You are either right or wrong. The problem of self-righteousness is a terrible mental problem. It creates a situation where the more intellectually educated you are, the more important it is for you to be right and to make sure that the other guy is wrong. Out of that we have a culture of adversarial thinking. Everybody is either for you or against you, and most people are against you. You are always hoping that somebody else will be wrong, and you try to help them to become wrong, because then you can be right. Can you imagine all the psychological problems that can flow out of this way of seeing? It is a way of seeing.

Student: I thought this week that every kind of religion thinks they are right and everybody else is wrong.

Dr. Hora: You are going to hell.

Student: They see God up there who thinks their religion is right. Whatever religion this person is, that's who God is and only taking care of, and that is what you are taught from the time you are born.

Dr. Hora: That is the tragedy of the rest of civilization. When Jesus said, "Judge not by the appearance but judge righteous judgment" (John 7:24), how many people understand this? Most people think you are either right or wrong. You judge what you see. It looks like there are some people who are right and there are some people who are wrong. Some people are Catholics and some people go to hell. You judge by appearances and they actually say this.

Student: And to make it even more complicated, in each religion there are four or five different groups who all think that they interpret it properly and everybody else doesn't.

Dr. Hora: Karl Marx has taken this all the way to absurdity. He called it dialectic materialism, and divided the world into two parts: the proletariat and the capitalists. The capitalists are wrong. Therefore the capitalists have to be annihilated by a process called class warfare.

In today's *New York Times*, there is a picture of a Muslim religious leader surrounded by people. This is an Egyptian, high-level Muslim person in power. You wouldn't believe it. He says that there are only the religious and those that are not submitting to the religious laws. There are Christians and other groups in Egypt. Now he says they cannot co-exist and therefore the non-religious have to be eliminated. Clearly, they have to be eliminated. It's like the Nazis. Whoever was not a pure-blooded Nazi had to be eliminated, and this Egyptian now in front of the whole world, in the American newspaper, makes this statement that the non-religious Muslims must be eliminated because the two cannot coexist.

This kind of radicalism is as mistaken as the Marxist ideology of dialectic materialism. Dialectic means you are either wrong or right. It is a dialectic process when the right and the wrong ideas are at war and the right ideas have to win. Marx and Engels determined what the right ideas are. The proletariat is the right idea and the capitalists are the wrong idea. That is a very simple philosophy. Look what catastrophic consequences this kind of thinking has brought about. Millions of people died because a few intellectuals called themselves philosophers, have written books about it and perpetuated this idea that there are only two ways you can look at life: right and wrong. If you happen to be on the wrong side, you have to be eliminated. Apparently in Yugoslavia the Serbs are doing this to the Muslims, and here in Egypt the Muslims are hoping to do this to the Christians, and the Jews are doing it to themselves. The Jews are very intolerant of each other, extremely so. The Muslims are dividing the world among the Muslims — the Islamics and the non-Islamics. The Nazis divided the world between the Aryans and the non-Aryans. There is always this division. In Yugoslavia they are also polarizing the whole area between the Serbs and Croatians. There are always politicians who cannot see the transcendent reality. They are constantly polarizing and trying to profit from dividing people along various (either religious or political or racial) lines. There are people who say all blacks have to be annihilated. There are blacks who say all whites have to be annihilated. It is a way of seeing reality. It's disastrous because of the dualistic thinking which breeds intolerance, hostility, and rivalry. It is tragic.

Here comes Jesus Christ and says it is good to be good. Actually Hora said that, but it's still valid. There is so much intolerance in the world that for most people it would be inconceivable that people could live together without animosity. Beyond Jesus Christ, there was only one man in recent history who offered a solution to the racial antagonism in the world. Who was this man? Nobody has an answer to this dilemma because Jesus Christ has been discredited by religion. Philosophers have been discredited by the blindness of the philosophers. There was one man in recent history that had an answer but nobody listened. Who was this man? He was Albert Schweitzer. Albert Schweitzer looked at the world and he saw the hopeless, tragic condition, and saw the vital importance of having reverence for life. Then all the hostilities and problems of intolerance would disappear, because people would disappear from our preoccupations, and we would have reverence for life. So, Albert Schweitzer was the only one who came up with an answer. It is neither heeded nor listened to; and if you do listen, you don't understand. When he was alive, not so long ago, people liked him. He got the Nobel prize and all kinds of recognition. He worked in Africa as a medical doctor, and was a Catholic, mind you. But he introduced his own philosophy, which was reverence for life. It was very pleasant to hear, but you don't hear any more about Albert Schweitzer. You ask somebody, "Who is that?" "I don't know." He went unheeded and he is already mostly forgotten.

Student: Is the purpose of the animals or life forms just to help us appreciate the multitude of forms and life?

Dr. Hora: We cannot say that is the purpose, but that is what appears to be. And God certainly loves the deer in the forest and the animals. Animals have a meaning just like nature, beauty, forests and mountains. They all have a meaning. God's creation of the universe elevates consciousness to gratitude and inspires with the beauty of that creation. But when we are confronted with intolerance — whether it is religious, racial or political intolerance like Communism, Islam, Judaism, and Catholicism — we observe that all of these various religions never even attempted to find a solution to the misery in the lives of people. If the world would understand Schweitzer's philosophy, there would be no need for intolerance anymore. He doesn't say love thy neighbor as thyself. He says you cannot love your neighbor because then you love somebody else. But you can revere his life. You can have reverence for life and then we wouldn't hurt a fly and there would be peace. The way the world is and was for many years, is that everybody hates everybody else — man's inhumanity to man.

Student: Sometimes it's hard to imagine yourself in the context of the world at large. I know that when I am away from home and I am losing joy or a loving outlook on life, it's very important to find the meaning of it and to be healed of it. Now how does the world manage? First of all I don't think it's very important to find the meaning. I mean people don't know there is a meaning to these things, and they are not searching for the healing or the spiritual remedy. What are they thinking and how do they live on a daily basis? You know I feel as if I am living in a protected kind of environment because I have the opportunity to be healed every time I go off in consciousness from a valid perspective. But what goes on in most people's thoughts? How can they stand it?

Dr. Hora: Well, people are polarizing their view of life — "this I like, this I don't like" — liking and not liking.

Student: When you are thinking that way, and you are thinking in a judgmental way, and you are thinking maliciously, you get sick.

Dr. Hora: Well it's a virus. If you get sick, it's the virus that made you sick. That is the belief. The doctors have told you that you get sick from virus or bacteria or climate or diet. You don't get sick from wrong thinking. Not many people are willing to face up to that.

Student: But that is the way it is. Most of the people in the world don't have an inkling about meaning or anything that we have been blessed to learn. So that is where the sickness is. I mean, everyone is sick.

Dr. Hora: Yes, there is an article in today's newspaper where somebody accuses the powers that be of inventing AIDS and inflicting it on people, and anybody who believes in it will get it. But that is silly because that is one idea. Life is a variety of all kinds of potential interactions and false beliefs. It is endless. You cannot limit it to one particular epidemic. But some people are beginning to think that maybe these terrible illnesses don't just arise out of nothing, that there is some evil thinking in the world that hypnotizes. People get hypnotized by political propaganda and economic interests. There are many people who get contaminated. The Nazis and Communists and millions of people begin to believe that this is the truth. The proletariat is the truth and they destroy capitalists. Similarly with anti-Semitism. Six million Jews were eliminated because there was one man, Hitler, who spread a rumor that the Jews were the cause of all evil in the world, and this kind of mental influence and propaganda was accepted by many millions of people. We see in families that they develop all kind of animosities, hostilities and hatred. It happens also in nations and it can become global.

Now today we have a global epidemic of AIDS. How did it come about? We never heard of this before. Suddenly millions of people are dying and they spend lots of money on research and they try to find something to blame it on. So it's a virus. You can't stop the virus. You can think about it but it doesn't lead anywhere. AIDS will kill millions of people until people find something else. It must be polio or tuberculosis. There is always an invisible enemy which releases all the accumulated hatreds and kills people, and the only way it will disappear is when something else comes along to replace it. And suddenly there will be no more AIDS. They come and they do their dirty work and then they disappear, being replaced by something else. This is the terrible world of human ignorance resulting from judging by appearances. The human species has a predilection to judge by appearances and to dualistic thinking like right and wrong, black and white, or this and that. This will persist as long as mankind fails to understand what Jesus taught and what Schweitzer taught, and what some other individuals, of whom we have not yet heard, taught. Not many people have heard of Metapsychiatry... right? So the world is suffering and life is difficult and dangerous. It is short but dirty. (laughing) If you are conscious of the philosophy of the reverence for life, that helps you to rise above interaction thinking, because in interaction thinking we think of people, and that is the problem. If you are imbued with the philosophy of reverence for life, you are not thinking of people. You are thinking of life and that is a great relief. There are no enemies. Life is not our enemy. It is God, the good. So the Third Principle says: "There is no interaction anywhere; there is only Omniaction everywhere." That is reverence for life. There is only life and we have to cherish it.

Student: How is it that everything is so one-sided and negative?

Dr. Hora: Everything is two-sided, and that is the problem.

Student: The interest is in being two-sided. What we describe here is so inspiring and the world sees everything as being conflict, and that is being broadcast globally.

Dr. Hora: It's the two-sided view of life — the good and the bad, the right and the wrong, the Jew and the Christian, the Islamic and Mohammad, the Pakistanis and the Bangladesh and the this and that. The problem is dualistic thinking. In interaction there is dualism. There is one and the other, self and other — relationships. You hear the psychologists talking about relationships. You have to establish a good relationship with somebody and get married and then you kill each other. (laughter)

I just recently had a chance to see a movie. Most people had seen it but I never even heard about it. It was by Woody Allen. He made this movie; he wrote it and he directed it. It is called *Husbands and Wives*. Do you know this movie? It's a terrible movie. All these young well-to-do people are constantly killing each other, marrying and divorcing and establishing relationships and breaking up the relationships. Everybody is constantly miserable with each other. Finally, Woody Allen achieves tremendous insight and he gets rid of his wife and says: I am alone now, I am okay: I will live like that for a while. It is so difficult in our culture. We are always working on our relationships, trying to make a go of it, and in the process, things get destroyed.

Student: So if you have a problem, you can say, in general, that anything that will help you focus your attention on life or God or some large...

Dr. Hora: Like an elephant. (laughter)

Student: Some, valid, large principle... and it doesn't really matter much how you get there — right? — in a non-dual perspective — some healing of some kind.

Dr. Hora: Right. The non-dual perspective on life.

Student: No matter what the problem really is, that is the healing.

Dr. Hora: Yes, that is the harmonizing principle of the universe. God says: "I am that I am" (Exodus 3:14) and "...besides me there is none else" (Isaiah 45:5). There is no other God but one God. "Hear O Israel: the Lord our God is one Lord," says the Bible (Deuteronomy 6:4). It is a non-dual God. The idea was to lift people out of the dualistic mode of thinking that is so troublesome.

Student: What's the difference between that and the idea that I have heard that illness, say AIDS or anything, is a type of punishment for two individuals for having the wrong thoughts?

Dr. Hora: Having sex?

Student: Or the wrong deeds, or the idea that nothing comes into experience uninvited (seventh principle). Is it that one focuses on ideas and one on the person?

Dr. Hora: Your question is not clear. You want to know if suffering is a sign of punishment?

Student: Well, I have heard that expressed. Many people say you are being punished for...

Dr. Hora: That is a religious fantasy. God is Love. How can He punish anybody? There is no such thing as punishment. There is such a thing as the suffering which afflicts the ignorant, and one ignorance is afflicting another ignorance. In the dualistic world view, man is seeking to have a relationship, either good or bad. They claim that they want a good relationship and invariably it turns bad because of the dualistic view of life. You cannot have a coin which has only one side. Every coin has to have two sides. So if you are looking for a good relationship, you will not be able to sustain it without a reversal. It is impossible. Everybody you talk to, whether married or unmarried, is looking for a good relationship, and that's a tragedy of mankind. It is not punishment. It is disaster. Nobody is punishing anybody. We are suffering because we are ignorant. Whatever bad happens to us, we had something to do with it in terms of the world view of seeing life in dualistic terms and judging life by appearances. So it is the sea of mental garbage. God does not afflict, because God is Love-Intelligence.

Student: Dr. Hora, if we find ourselves thinking in terms of harmony in a life with somebody vs. a reverence for life, is there always going to be a problem if we think in terms of relationship? That is the essence of life with relationship?

Dr. Hora: Yes. Everybody wants that. Everybody wants to find a companion with whom he will be able to maintain a harmonious relationship. It doesn't last longer than getting to the subway or the corner of Seventy-Second Street.

Student: So if we think in terms of reverence for life, there is no this one or that one.

Dr. Hora: There is just joint participation in the good of God. What are you laughing at?

Student: Judging by appearances has been giving me a lot of trouble lately.

Dr. Hora: Well, hopefully this might open your eyes to see that you are not in a relationship and you are not a loner. It is not valid to be a loner and it is not valid to be in a relationship. It is valid to have reverence for life and to be a transparency for God. God is life. Life is God, and we revere it. We are grateful for it. It is intelligence that pervades the whole universe, and is guiding us and guarding us and governing us all the way. God, good, guides, guards, and governs (laughter) — five Gs.

Remember once we had a conference on Albert Schweitzer? None of these things came out. Nobody wrote it up.

Student: The conference was called "Reverence for Life."

Dr. Hora: Yes, and we haven't learned anything. There are some conferences where you don't learn anything because the participants don't know it. (laughing) We had a very strange kind of conference.

Other books by Thomas Hora

Encounters with Wisdom: Book One

This book is the first of a series of short volumes that present Dr. Thomas Hora's Metapsychiatric teachings through dialogues with his students.

Contents: Spiritual Blessedness ~ The Inside and the Outside ~ Death and Mourning ~ The Meaning of Attachment ~ Abundance ~ What Yen Hui Understood ~ Koans and the Rosetta Stone of Metapsychiatry ~ Spontaneity

135 pages / $12.00 / ISBN 1-931052-03-4

Dialogues in Metapsychiatry

These dialogues between Dr. Hora and his students shed new light on what is real and what is illusory, and on such issues as our purpose in life, the good of life, affluence, ambition, anxiety, humility, freedom, safety, and joy.

Contents: The Supreme Way ~ The Perfect Principle ~ The Real ~ The Right Context ~ Thinking and Knowing ~ I Am the Light ~ Meditation ~ Affluence ~ Who Is in Control? ~ What Is Good? ~ Beholding the Good ~ What Is Beholding? ~ Beyond Religion ~ Symbolic Structures ~ What Is a Healing? ~ Freedom and Joy ~ Safety ~ Protection ~ Substance ~ Parasitism ~ Self-Pity ~ Pleasure and Joy ~ Frictionlessness ~ The Human Mockery ~ Eternal Damnation ~ What Is the Purpose of Man? ~ What Is Life? ~ Overcoming the World ~ Ambition ~ The Gatekeeper ~ Meekness and Humility ~ Is God Slow? ~ Anxiety ~ Believing and Knowing ~ Indestructible Life ~ Self-Confirmatory Ideation ~ Power Struggle ~ What Is Hypnotism? ~ Progress ~ Is It Worth It? ~ Completeness ~ Self-Esteem ~ Interaction or Omniaction? ~ Innocence ~ Yes Is Good ~ No Is Also Good ~ On Being Helpful ~ Parameters of Progress ~ Reading List and Index

248 pages / $14.95 / ISBN 0-8245-1637-0

Existential Metapsychiatry

A companion to *Dialogues in Metapsychiatry*, it is dedicated to "the sincere seekers after the truth who are willing to forego intellectual conformity in exchange for freedom and authenticity. . . . Dr. Hora presents a therapeutic method based upon the free use of creative intelligence and open-minded receptivity to the patient. His therapy leaves behind all preconceived ideas, explanations, and speculations, especially those based upon cause and effect reasoning. Instead he participates with the patient in a search for truth and understanding resulting in healing and harmony with the fundamental order of existence." (Excerpt from book cover)

Contents: Basic Concepts ~ Existential Validation ~ Commitment ~ The Prayer of Beholding ~ The Transpersonal ~ Operationalism ~ Compassion ~ Believing and Disbelieving ~ Love-Intelligence ~ Nihilation ~ Competition ~ Laws and Principles ~ The Right Question ~ The Realm of the Non-Dual ~ Personhood ~ Needs ~ Family Therapy ~ Ethics of Psychotherapy ~ What Are Thoughts? ~ Conscious Union with God ~ The Epistemology of Believing ~ A Case of Phobia ~ Fulfillment ~ Ego-Gratification or Existential Fulfillment? ~ Romantic Love and Spiritual Love ~ "I Am" ~ Healing of Character ~ Identity and Individuality ~ The Clinical Eye ~ Context ~ Dynamics of Depression ~ The Divine Marriage ~ The Serpent ~ The Pearl of Great Price ~ As Thou Seest ~ Influencing ~ Reading List

234 pages / $20.00 / ISBN 0-913105-007

One Mind:
A Psychiatrist's Spiritual Teachings

"The meaning of life is to come to know Reality."

– Thomas Hora, M.D.

These dialogues between Dr. Hora and his students first teach us the meaning of our mental, emotional and physical problems, and then point to the Reality of God, the one true Mind in which we live and move and have our being. As we become aware of our true existence in God, our problems begin to dissolve and we realize peace, assurance, gratitude and love. Those who are familiar with these teachings and those who are new to them will appreciate and benefit from the inspired wisdom in One Mind.

Contents: One Mind ~ The Dynamics of Liberation ~ A Sermon in the Flesh ~ Hype ~ Beyond Words ~ The Mystery of Ignorance ~ The Gift of Knowledge and Speech ~ Basket Weaving ~ Receptivity ~ Glowing ~ Self-Esteem ~ God Is ~ Epistemology ~ The Right Orientation ~ Pain and Gratitude ~ Heaven ~ The Herodian Thought ~ Envy ~ Awareness ~ What Is Thinking? ~ Freedom ~ The Millennial Vision ~ Pain ~ The Serpent and the Dove ~ Noah's Ark ~ "Take My Yoke..." ~ Existentially Engaged ~ Humility ~ Real Communication: God to Man ~ Immunity ~ The Universe Speaks ~ Infinite Structure ~ Possessiveness ~ Collective Right-Knowing ~ Attachments ~ The Mystery of Evil ~ Work ~ Progress ~ Overcoming Self-Confirmation ~ Life, Love, Laughter, and Listening ~ Mental Arm-Wrestling ~ The Eleven Principles of Metapsychiatry ~ Published Works of Thomas Hora, M.D. ~ Index

400 pages / $25.00 / ISBN 1-931052-01-8

Beyond the Dream:
Awakening to Reality

"*Beyond the Dream* contains original insights on life, health, healing, and wholeness ... insights that can help anyone to awaken spiritually — to find light beyond the dream of life as personal selfhood. Dr. Hora drew on the teachings of Jesus as much as he did on conventional psychotherapy to evolve a way of seeing and being in the world that bears good fruit, here and now.

Contents: What Is Man? ~ Phenomenology and Hermeneutics ~ Thoughts and Feelings ~ Thought as Energy ~ Shouldlessness ~ The Law of Karma ~ What Can Be Done and What Cannot Be Done ~ Prepare Ye the Way ~ The Curtain of Time ~ Time and Timelessness ~ "He That Hath an Ear" ~ Information and Transformation ~ The Teacher and the Teaching ~ Beyond Nothingness ~ Transubstantiation ~ Willfulness ~ "Fail-Safe" ~ A Sense of Humor ~ The Curtain of Fear ~ Sex Education ~ Yielding ~ The Natural, the Supernatural, and the Spiritual ~ Innocence ~ The Bureaucrat and the Therapist ~ Safety ~ Marriage and Parenting ~ The Divine Context ~ "The Nightmare Pill" ~ Fearlessness ~ The Love of Being Loving ~ The Healing Environment ~ The Riddle of the Sphinx ~ Approbation ~ The Question of Affectivity ~ The Physical Is Mental ~ The Healing Factor ~ Malicious Hypnotism ~ Semantics ~ The Body ~ Anger ~ Alcoholism ~ Levels of Cognitive Integration ~ Friction ~ The Other Cheek ~ Anxiety ~ The Origin of Man ~ The Line and the Circle ~ Enlightenment ~ Solitary Man ~ Decision or Commitment? ~ Guilt ~ Evil ~ Compassion ~ Is There Nothingness? ~ The "IS" ~ How Mature Is God? ~ The Living Soul ~ Prayer of "At-one-ment" ~ Reading List and Index

348 pages / $16.95 / ISBN 0-8245-1636-2

In Quest of Wholeness

Seminal early writings of Dr. Hora on the foundations of Metapsychiatry.

Contents: Cognition and Health ~ Illness and Health — What Are They? ~ The Transpersonal Perspective ~ Beyond Self ~ Responsibility ~ Wholeness ~ Prayer ~ Identity ~ The Epistemology of Love ~ Commentary on a Lecture at a Scientific Meeting ~ Religious Values in Illness and Health ~ Transcendence and Healing ~ Existential Psychotherapy, Basic Principles ~ Bibliography and Index

141 pages / $15.00 / ISBN 1-931-052-02-6

To order or for more information
please call (860) 434-2999
FAX (860) 434-1512
or e-mail *PAGLBooks@aol.com*
Thank you for reading *Encounters in Wisdom: Book II.*
We hope you found it beneficial.